Mental Training for Runners – How to Stay Motivated

Melanie

Stay Positive !

Mental Training for Runners
How to Stay Motivated

Jeff Galloway

Meyer & Meyer Sport

British Library Cataloguing in Publication Data
A catalogue record for this book is available from the British Library

Jeff Galloway
Mental Training for Runners – How to Stay Motivated
Maidenhead: Meyer & Meyer Sport (UK) Ltd., 2011
ISBN 978-1-84126-315-1

© 2011 Meyer & Meyer Sport (UK) Ltd.
Auckland, Beirut, Budapest, Cairo, Cape Town, Dubai, Graz, Indianapolis, Maidenhead,
Melbourne, Olten, Singapore, Tehran, Toronto
Member of the World
Sport Publishers' Association (WSPA)
www.w-s-p-a.org

Printed and bound by: B.O.S.S Druck und Medien GmbH, Germany
ISBN 978-1-84126-315-1
E-Mail: info@m-m-sports.com
www.m-m-sports.com

Contents

1 Your Inner Strength – Believe In It!

You have within yourself the power to overcome low motivation on the lowest energy days, and the power to accomplish any realistic goal if you are willing to follow a successful plan. With the right balance of stress and rest, including physical and mental training, you can be prepared for any goal. On race day, using a strategy that you believe in, you can gain control over your attitude, energy level, motivation, and success.

You've already started the journey. Most of those I've surveyed, who have been running for 5 years or more, tell me that they have a better attitude, handle stress better, and are generally more happy than they were before they started running. Most runners (and especially family members of runners) will admit that after a run they have a much better outlook on life, are nicer to others and handle stress better. What is going on here?

A gentle paced run activates attitude-boosting hormones that can instantly transmit good feelings throughout your body. Within a few minutes, you feel better, more relaxed, have more energy and experience the powerful internal confidence that comes when the body and spirit are working as a team.

With the help of my wife Barbara, who wrote the forward to this book, I've discovered nuggets of research that have helped me understand why some runners stay motivated and some do not, why some perform well and others don't and why some enjoy their training and others take it like medicine. Scientists Candace Pert, PhD, and Bruce Lipton, PhD, explain the biological and molecular changes that allow us to control our emotions and restructure negative behavior patterns in the subconscious. John Sarno, MD, has shown through his methods that chronic pain, sometimes experienced for years, may be reduced or eliminated. I have found that both injured and uninjured runners can improve motivation and perform better when they apply his methods.

For three decades, I've been researching, trying motivational strategies, tabulating results and learning from experience. The ideas in this book are the latest evolution of a method that has been practiced successfully by thousands. I offer these ideas as one runner to another and as my opinions. As always, seek medical advice for health issues from those who specialize in the area of your issue – especially find someone who wants to find a way for you to continue running.

You can do it!

Jeff Galloway

2 To Be Happy, Joyous, Confident

By Barbara Galloway

When Jeff told me that he was writing a book on motivation, my first thought was "For what do you want to be motivated?" Most runners have several or several dozen reasons to be and stay motivated. For me, the answer is in the title of this preface. I want to be a happy, joyous, and confident animal.

The late Dr. George Sheehan, cardiologist, philosopher and *Runner's World* columnist told us to "Be first a good animal." There is a lot of satisfaction when we follow our most natural patterns of exertion – to move, walk and run. At a fast pace, there are more aches, pains and fatigue. But when you choose a relaxing pace, with the right balance of running and walking, you can be a good, happy, and joyous animal.

I believe that George was telling us that we have within ourselves all that we need for happiness. By using our body regularly and communicating with our spirit, we can be healthy and active. Positive things happen when we are first and foremost good, active animals.

For many years, this has been my ultimate motivation. But, like many experiences in life, running begs us to dig deeper. I have made it a mission to search for ideas that can enhance motivation to exercise and to share these with Jeff. The ideas presented in this book have enriched our running experiences, and I hope that you will experience similar benefits.

I'm not going to stop looking. There are so many great ideas, experiences, and opportunities out there.

Get motivated, stay motivated!

Barbara Galloway

3   The Ultimate Source of Motivation

At the age of 13, I was a very overweight, lazy kid. I wasn't proud of being fat and realized that exercise could be a key to losing my extra baggage. But in my internal priority list, far ahead of being lean was the avoidance of exercise. I now know that I had programmed myself to believe that it hurt.

What changed was a school requirement that every boy be on a sport team after school. Generally, I'm not a fan of forcing kids to exercise, but it worked for me because of the spontaneous fun that emerged from almost every run with the cross country team. The head coach, Paul Koshewa, was the most lenient among coaches and allowed us "options." I initially joined a group of other lazy kids who would jog 200 yards to the woods and goof off.

But one day, an older kid that I liked said, "Galloway, you're coming with us today." My anxiety soared because these kids actually ran long distances – 3 miles! I had my lazy boy strategy in place: When I reached the protective cover of the woods I would grab my leg, claim I was injured, and throw rocks in the creek. But the runners started telling jokes and then gossip about the teachers. I listened at first, huffing and puffing. With a little more fitness, I began to participate in the conversations. We shared stories, argued, and more than anything else, enjoyed the fun environment that we created each day.

Within 10 weeks, I was hooked on the endorphin experience, and still am ... over half a century later. My grades significantly improved. I discovered that even when things had not been going well at school or personally, the workout with my group turned my mind, body and spirit around. But there was something more powerful about the running experience that pulled me out on the roads and trails by myself when the school year ended. The same force was at work years later when my Navy ship pulled into port after 3 weeks at sea and I found myself wanting to run before I did anything else.

I believe that as the frontal lobe of the brain evolved to give us judgement and perspective, humans have been searching for meaning in life. When we perform certain positive activities, we stimulate biological changes to occur that make us feel good about ourselves and about the quality of our life. Each day, as we weave a series of these experiences, such as aerobic exercise, helping others, performing productive work, our actions stimulate the release of natural, mood-altering substances. An amazing network of receptor molecules sends and receives the signals from these hormones throughout the body and mind. Running is one of the best ways to trigger the production of these peptides that tell us that things are going to be OK, that we sense there is hope, that we feel good.

When I've had to sort through problems and general "life junk," the only action I have found that can diffuse most of the negative and leave me with a positive attitude, is a gentle run. Research shows that after a 30-minute aerobic run, the mind is sharper and the problem-solving frontal cortex is activated. Even when I'm stressed before the start, after the first five minutes on almost every gentle run, the tide shifts to a positive mindset, thinking is focused, and motivation improves. From the first day I ran aerobically, I have intuitively known that running was allowing good things to happen.

My greatest joy today is helping others find this joy and grow through the fitness empowerment journey. I've become a student of this process, and this book will describe what I have discovered so far. Simply stated, I believe that each of us can set up a training program for the body and the mind that gives one control over attitude. Every day runners tell me that running has improved their self worth, helping them understand who they are. As the months go by, they increasingly like what they feel and see. Then they tell me about accomplishments that would not have been possible under their pre-run thought patterns.

When there is balance in pacing, rest days, and challenging workouts, we come away from a run as happier people. I don't believe that we can be happy all the time. But I believe that running allows the body, mind and spirit to deal with challenges, making us feel "whole."

As we activate this boost of the spirit, day after day, we become part of a larger force: that there is meaning to our existence. During each run, we have the opportunity to expand the benefits in so many directions.

So, get out there and run!

4 Glossary of Mind-Body Elements

There are a number of body systems, networks, substances, etc., that are constantly monitoring external and internal stress and capabilities, keeping all of the systems working. How they interact will determine which substances are secreted into the receptor molecules that affect your current emotions and your current level of motivation. The following components are described in a conceptual format so that you can glimpse into the workings of this marvelous system.

Mind – An interconnected information system throughout the body with communication transmission going on constantly as information hormones (peptides) lock into receptors on billions of cells. The reflex, subconscious brain monitors this flow of information and has programmed responses for specific stimuli. The frontal lobe and the right brain can be separately activated when conscious control is needed. When emotions are balanced and positive, the preprogramming has been somewhat consistent and realistic, the system runs smoothly and almost automatically.

Brain – Located in your head, this complex is composed of many components that are constantly processing information. Some are connected in circuits that can work together, and some work separately. There are logical networks and creative ones. The frontal lobe allows humans the ability to take control after monitoring patterns and deciding to change behaviors to get something done.

The Reflex Brain (Subconscious) – A more primitive area where stimulus-response actions are programmed. Ancient patterns are embedded, which ensured survival long ago, along with programming from childhood. When we learn a new activity by doing it over and over again, we can program this reflex brain to perform automatic patterns of behavior. Here is how Bruce Lipton, PhD, describes this entity: "In reality, the subconscious is an emotionless database of stored programs whose function is strictly concerned with reading environmental signals and engaging in hardwired behavioral programs, no questions asked, no judgments made."[1]

Frontal Lobe (conscious brain) – This "newer" part of the brain allows humans to understand, plan and enjoy what they are doing, develop strategy, make decisions and search for and understand complex thoughts, experiences, and emotions.

Left Brain – Located in the frontal cortex, this circuit connects components of logic, judgment, language, math, and other areas. The conscious part of the left brain can take control over our reflex brain.

Right Brain – This nonverbal, unconscious circuit connects areas of creativity and intuition. Mental training techniques can empower the right brain to find creative solutions, tap hidden resources, and allow you to do what you are capable of doing – even if you don't know that you are capable of doing so.

Conditioning for reflex actions – The control part of the frontal lobe can program the subconscious reflex brain to conduct habitual activities. During the first few times we ride a bicycle, for example, the frontal lobe consciously (and usually awkwardly) drives the body through a series of actions. By repeating the same behavior patterns regularly, reflex patterns are established and riding the bicycle becomes more and more automatic. The reflex brain then subconsciously conducts the patterns that allow us to ride a bike. "The subconscious reflex mind is a programmable hard drive into which our life experiences are downloaded. The programs are fundamentally stimulus-response behaviors." [2]

Receptors – Specialized molecules on the surface of a cell where ligands (hormones, drugs and other substances) can bind so that information can be sent and received – very quickly – throughout body and mind.

Ligands – Substances (hormones, drugs, etc.) secreted by the body that bind to the molecule receptors and send and receive information, about emotions, beliefs, behaviors, etc., that can change our attitude.

Peptides – Ligands that connect the communication system. In the words of Candice Pert, PhD, "Peptides serve to weave the body's organs and systems into a single web that reacts to both internal and external environmental changes with complex, subtly orchestrated responses."[3]

TMS (Tension myositis syndrome) – When the reflex brain becomes overloaded with stress/pressure, it subconsciously controls a reduction in blood flow to areas that have been damaged. The resulting pain is much greater than it normally would be for the amount of damage. By taking control by conscious thought, one can reduce stress and open up blood flow – managing or eliminating the pain (John Sarno, MD, *Healing Back Pain*, or *Mind-body Prescription*).

Growth Mode – under normal conditions, when under "normal stress" for the individual, the reflex brain keeps all functions going, rebuilds damaged areas, replaces worn cells, produces needed energy, removes waste, etc. Peptides that are produced tell the body/mind that you feel fine, things are good.

Protection Mode – When stress increases to a high level, the reflex brain protects itself and the organism by increasing blood flow to the limbs and to the reflex brain itself. At the same time, blood flow is constricted to the frontal lobe, digestive, immune and waste removal systems. For a short period, the muscles can work at a higher level of activity. This allowed our ancestors to survive threats and can keep us running at a high level of performance until the resources run out. Then there is an extended recovery time needed. Triggered also by protection stress are hormones, such as cortisol, which aid in recovery and healing, but are also linked to depression and low motivation.

1: Bruce Lipton, PhD, *Biology of Belief*, p. 135.
2: Bruce Lipton, PhD, *Biology of Belief*, p. 135.
3: Candace Pert, PhD, *Molecules of Emotion*, p. 148.

5 The Mind and Body Are Connected

Your mind-body information network sends messages in seconds that control your motivation

At any moment in time, you have a continuous flow of information from billions of cells throughout your body and mind. The signals they send can determine negative or positive reactions in your brain and throughout your body, stimulating the production of attitude-changing hormones, which determine how motivated you will feel.

Candace Pert, PhD, in her informative book *Molecules Of Emotion,* explains how the brain is "extremely well connected" to the rest of the body at a molecular level "so much so that the term mobile brain is an apt description of the psychosomatic network through which intelligent information travels from one system to another." [4]

Secretions are constantly being produced due to current mental and physical conditions. Pert says that current feelings and beliefs will determine which of these peptide secretions are made. These substances lock onto the receptor molecules on the outer edge of most cells, sending information, giving directions and significantly affecting our motivation and energy level.

"Receptor molecules, on the outer edge of most cell membranes, are responsive to the outside environment with information substances such as hormones, antigens, drugs, peptides or neurotransmitters. The information processing occurs at the receptor where the signal to the cell can be modulated by the action of other receptors, the physiology of the cell and even past events and memories of them." [5]

"Peptides serve to weave the body's organs and systems into a single web that reacts to both internal and external environmental changes with complex subtly orchestrated responses." [6]

So the old concept that the mind is separate from the body is not correct, according to the research. Here is what Bruce Lipton says about this new approach:

"This new perspective on human biology does not view the body as just a mechanical device, but incorporates the role of mind and spirit. This breakthrough in the science of biology is fundamental to healing for it shows us that when we change our perceptions or beliefs we send totally different messages to our cells. In effect, we reprogram them. This new biology reveals why people can have spontaneous remissions or recover from injuries thought to be permanent disabilities." [7]

For more than three decades, I have believed and written that running brings together body, mind and spirit better than any other activity I have researched or experienced. Candace Pert, PhD, Bruce Lipton, Phd, and John Sarno, MD, have analyzed the internal connections throughout our bodies and have helped me understand the biological and mental framework that can be used to boost our motivation, and tap into our potential.

Here's how Candace Pert explains why we feel so good after "playing" (such as during a good run): "When we are playing, we are stretching our emotional expressive ranges, loosening up our biochemical flow of information, getting unstuck, and healing our feelings." [8]

The mind is a very powerful network of information transmitters embedded throughout the body, connecting most cells. Mental training techniques can harness this powerful system by managing stress and sending positive messages. These actions stimulate positive secretions, which can change attitude within a few moments. Let's see how the marvelous mind works.

The reflex brain monitors constant flow of information, monitors stress and engages protection mode when stress is too high.

The subconscious reflex brain is a powerful part of the brainstem that keeps the basic services running: heart, lungs, blood flow, etc. In additon, it has countless actions and thoughts in memory, programmed to respond to perceived stress and threats.

When "things aren't right" due to physical or psychological events, or the overall stress level from all sources is too high, the reflex brain goes into a "protection mode" and triggers secretions that lower our motivation to do activities that add stress (such as running on a lazy day or maintaining a hard pace when the effort level is uncomfortable). If no conscious action is taken, this subconscious reflex center will reduce blood flow to the digestive system, waste removal system, immune system, and frontal lobe.

By some simple conscious mental focus actions, you can use the frontal lobe to override the reflex brain. By following a proven method, as shown in the mental training section of this book, you can lower your stress level, reducing the negative attitude secretions. Regular mental training will reprogram the reflex brain for any realistic challenge, while setting up patterns for pushing past barriers, maximizing performance, and even reducing chronic pain. Training can also help you access the right brain, which unlocks intuitive sources of inner strength, conserves energy, and initiates creative solutions to problems.

To understand how the reflex brain is programmed, let's use the experience of learning to ride a bicycle. During the first few rides, the frontal lobe takes conscious control, moving us from one step to the next, over and over again, until the pattern has been repeated enough times to be hardwired into the reflex brain. At that point, riding a bike will be coordinated automatically and subconsciously, enabling us to engage in conscious thought in other areas at the same time we are peddling down the road.

When we are young, we learn many behavior patterns that become embedded into the reflex brain. Some are helpful and some are counterproductive later in life. For example, many young runners learn in PE class or in high school sports that they should not walk when they run, that walking is "failure." This is hardwired in many adults who try to take up running and believe that the only way to be a successful runner is to run continuously. Most will reach a certain distance where they hit a fatigue wall or become injured because of this compulsion to run continuously. They feel like failures because they received in some bad programming.

Every year, thousands of former non-stop runners reprogram the reflex brain after reading one of my books, attending one of my retreats/schools/clinics or joining one of our training groups. The logical reason for taking strategic walk breaks is to activate the frontal lobe. Through the reinforcement of the members of a Galloway group or my instruction, they do it. The rewards of endorphins and a positive attitude boost allow them to push through the former wall, recover quickly, and often record faster times. A vibrating timer allows for the behavior to be repeated in the right pattern without thinking. The new behavior of run-walk-run becomes hardwired. I hear from dozens of former non-stop "failures" who cross the finish line of a marathon, half marathon, 10K or 5K with the most wonderful feeling of accomplishment experienced in their lives. The reprogramming is complete!

The actions of 1) taking charge over the reflex brain, 2) believing in the method, and 3) performing the mostly gentle training of mind and body, will activate the positive peptides, boost attitude and recondition the reflex brain.

4. Candace Pert, PhD, *Molecules of Emotion,* p. 188
5. Candace Pert, PhD, *Molecules of Emotion,* p. 352-353
6. Candace Pert, PhD, *Molecules of Emotion,* p. 148
7. Bruce Lipton, PhD, from the Forword to *Passage Of Change* by Nancy Marie
8. Candace Pert, PhD, *Molecules of Emotion,* p. 277

6   Why Do We Feel Unmotivated?

I believe that stress and pressure stimulate the reflex brain to trigger a series of subconscious actions that result in low motivation, burnout, pain, and loss of focus.

The reflex brain monitors total stress throughout your mind-body network. When total stress levels increases to a level that the reflex brain senses as "too high", it shifts into "protection mode" triggering a series of reactions to reduce motivation: sending negative messages, stimulating secretion of negative mood hormones, reducing blood flow to damaged areas – the frontal lobe brain, digestive tract and immune system.

Because blood flow is reduced to the gut, the brain's energy source, blood glucose, is reduced. Lower blood flow and lower fuel supply reduces the conscious brain's ability to take command, allowing the subconscious brain to stay in control.

Stress hormones are subconsciously triggered, and these lock into receptor molecules. Negative attitude messages are sent and received throughout the body-mind within a few minutes. If stress is not reduced and the reflex stays in control, there can be a downward trend of low motivation, doubt, depression, etc.

Pain! Many of your aches and pains may be the result of stress. The over-stressed subconscious reflex brain knows the location of current injuries and other damage because it is constantly receiving this information from areas all over the body. As the overall stress load increases (even due to anticipating a hard or tiring workout), the reflex brain will subconsciously reduce blood flow to these areas. This results in pain that would normally not be felt (or would be minimal and manageable without the reduction in blood flow). Dr. John Sarno covers this condition, tension myositis syndrome (TMS) in his books *The Mind-body Prescription* and *Healing Back Pain*. I highly recommend them.

Later in this book you will learn how you can turn your attitude around by taking conscious control, adjusting to realistic goals, setting up several different plans of action, believing in the plans and staying positive. You'll also learn how the mind-body can keep you going while managing stress.

Understanding the Sources of Stress/Pressure

Pressure is generated by perceived expectations. We know that our boss, spouse, parents, children, etc., each have expectations of various types. Most of this is not communicated, which is too bad. Things get more interesting as we interact with the key people in our lives and encounter conflicting expectations. In many cases, the expectations exceed what we can deliver, currently (or ever). Self-perceived pressure can produce the greatest stress for most of the runners with whom I've worked. Those who have perfectionist tendencies accumulate the most pressure. In any case, sustained pressure is a major source of stress. But there is hope.

Sources of Stress

Goal stress – Goals can motivate us to to run when we might otherwise sleep in and to push harder when we don't feel like doing so. But on the tough days, we often sense pressure from a looming goal and deadline. Choosing goals that are not realistic is a very common source of pressure and will make every aspect of the journey more stressful.

Workout stress – Extending the distance of long runs results in greater fatigue at the end. Heat increases this stress. Speed training offers an additional set of challenges. All of these can be managed, but the stress load will increase during the training and trigger low motivation hormones and other protection responses. Good news: In this book you'll find coping strategies for each of these stress sources.

"Exceeding our speed limit" stress – We usually feel really good at the beginning of the workout too good. The increased pace or extended distance or reduced run-walk-run ratio produces a gradual fatigue build-up that is often denied until the muscles are spent. This dramatically increases lingering soreness and muscle weakness for days afterward, which add to the stress load.

Lingering fatigue – When one is pushing past endurance or speed limits by increasing physical workload, most of the fatigue is erased during the rest day after workouts. When the workload was too hard for current ability and/or not enough rest was allowed, some body parts have pockets of lingering damage. The subconscious brain targets these areas for blood flow restriction when stress is too high (see the TMS section in the glossary).

Other Sources of Stress/Pressure:

Primitive genetic programming – Survival reflexes that were appropriate for hunter-gathers or cavemen, but not in our era (for example anger management issues).

Negative learning – Behavior patterns learned in childhood when we imitated parents, teachers, coaches who simply did not know the correct methods or concepts (or didn't know they were being imitated). Even when we learn that these early lessons were not logical or right, childhood programming will trigger anxieties when we embark on a positive method that is in conflict.

Unresolved issues from childhood/adolescence – very commonly due to anger and rage from early development: neglect, lack of love and caring, unresolved disputes, no respect, being told that one is a failure, etc.

Current stress from job, family, etc. – Most commonly these revolve around continuing life conflict situations that you cannot control. Some examples are the following: you have to work for a boss who makes bad decisions, you and your spouse disagree about some family issue; you want to give your kids some form of freedom but they are acting in suspicious ways.

Diffusing Stress/Pressure

Before we can reprogram the reflex brain and reach our potential for running enjoyment, we must deal with the situation. Each positive step you take will empower your conscious brain to take control away from the subconscious.

- You don't have to eliminate the stress to be motivated, but you must acknowledge it. Honesty is the best policy, and denial results in more stress later.
- You must acknowledge that stress is causing the loss of motivation/pain/loss of mental focus. Until you take conscious action to be aware of what is going on, the subconscious brain will control the situation, which will become more negative. Just a statement to yourself ("I am under stress, and I'm going to deal with it") is the first step that will engage the conscious frontal lobe to take control over subconscious reflex thoughts and actions.
- Each significant area of stress must be recognized for maximum stress reduction. Go over the list of stress sources in the section above, and focus on your prime suspects. Remember that you don't have to resolve the issue or eliminate it. Simply say to yourself that you know that these specific stresses are bothering you.

Positive Steps

1. Develop a coping strategy that allows the conscious left brain to override the subconscious reflex brain. Follow the plans in the "Mental Training" chapter. Just telling yourself that you have a plan and believing in the plan can change the secretions and start the positive emotional messages communicated throughout your mind-body.

2. Pressure can be acknowledged and managed by communicating with the people who have expectations of you. It is appropriate to ask the question: "What are your expectations of me in this area?" A simple conversation with key people can set up positive plans for understanding, adjusting, and then managing the expectations. Taking action in each area will continue go give you more control over the situation and improve attitude.

3. Through mental training, the subconscious reflex brain can be reprogrammed. In the "Mental Training" chapter, you will learn how to break up the former stressful challenges into a series of steps. This makes the task do-able, which continues to stimulate the positive secretions and allows the peptides transmit positive messages throughout the body's network.

4. Gentle running, with the right run-walk-run ratio, will produce endorphins. These create a positive shift by themselves. Endorphins are powerful attitude adjusters.

5. A series of positive actions generate momentum. The mind-body senses that things are improving, which lowers stress. Growth mode can kick in, which takes away the blood flow restrictions. Positive peptides lock into receptor molecules and transmit positive messages.

Tools That Give You Control

Most of the runners I've worked with on motivational issues have brought most of the stress on themselves. In many cases, the individual doesn't understand the principles of training or setting up a realistic goal. Listed below are the leading running sources of stress/pressure with the page(s) In this book where you can find solutions.

- **The goal is too challenging** – see the "Magic Mile" section on pp. 83-86. I ask beginners to run the first race "to finish." After the first one, a realistic improvement can be motivating. But when the goal is not realistic or at the edge of possibility, more stress is generated through doubt, uncertainty and the tough training needed to prepare for the goal. You can believe in the magic mile as a predictor of your best possible performance as noted in the section listed. Then you can make adjustments for non-ideal conditions. This puts you in charge, reducing stress, while promoting positive peptide production. The result: A better attitude.

- **Not being prepared for the race** – Having a long run of 26 miles before a marathon, compared with a long one of 22 miles or shorter, has dramatically improved motivation during the last month before the race and during the race (according to those who have tried it both ways). As you blend the elements into a team, you gain control over your destiny. This makes your belief stronger and improves positive attitude peptides and motivation.

- **Running too fast on long runs** – In my experience, the leading cause of injury and burnout among runners has been exceeding the speed limit on long ones or not taking walk breaks frequently enough. Most runners who do this don't know the pace is too fast. Runners who used to experience "burnout" by going too fast, usually improve attitude significantly by slowing down to a much more conservative pace. There is no benefit in running long runs faster, and I've not found a pace that is too slow. "I've found it best to run at least 2 minutes per mile slower on long runs, than one can currently run in a marathon. When in doubt, slow down even more."

- **Running too far before taking a walk break** – See the run-walk-run section on pp. 83-86. By taking walk breaks more frequently, you'll receive a better endorphin effect and reduce physical stress. On some days, the run segments can be adjusted according to how you feel. On long runs, take the most gentle ratio.

- **Low blood sugar** – Read the blood sugar boosting section on page 118. Low blood sugar is a major source of stress because this is your brain's only fuel source. The reflex brain monitors the level carefully and stimulates negative peptides when low. It's easy to boost the level.

- **Workout stress** – See the section on "leap of faith goal" on page 85. If the goal is too challenging for your current ability level, the speedwork will be too fast, and the results of races will be frustrating. This increases stress loads.

- **Injury symptoms and injury stress** – See the section on troubleshooting injuries, on page 134. Do your best to determine whether it's an injury or TMS (tension myositis syndrome). If it's an injury, you need to take at least 3-5 days off to start the healing and then reduce the training load to stay below the threshold of irritation. But the pain from your "weak links" could be TMS. This occurs when stress on the reflex brain reduces blood flow to these body parts, causing pain that is much greater than the damage would indicate. By acknowledging that stress is the cause, and letting the frontal lobe take charge, you can open the blood flow and keep training. As always, consult your doctor about medical issues.

The Stress of Top Performance
The more challenging the training, the greater the stress

Physical training can be motivating and bring us to the brink of top performance. But as the stress builds up, the reflex brain goes into "protection mode" shutting off blood flow and stimulating negative hormones that lock into molecules all over the body and mind. Successful world-class athletes have intuitively developed coping methods to keep going under the protection mode, and turn the attitude around under difficult and stressful conditions. The first step is having a plan to diffuse the stress.

At first, a challenging goal can increase motivation. But as the workouts get harder, the reflex brain sends anxieties and questions current capabilities – especially if this is a personal record. This sets up goal-related anxieties that trigger the release of negative motivation peptides resulting in a negative emotional mental environment.

Demanding workouts are necessary for top performance. But even those who love to push themselves to the limit in speed workouts experience more aches and pains and stress hormones that lower motivation. Lingering fatigue adds to the stress. When the body is pushed to its limits, the reflex brain initiates a protection mode response (see glossary). This causes a significant reduction of blood flow to the brain, the gut, and the immune system as blood flow is increased to the limbs. Corticosterone, a steroid hormone that is associated with depression and reduced motivation, is produced to repair damage.

- Messages from the reflox brain tell us that we are not ready for the effort
- Blood flow is constricted to areas of damage, causing pain or TMS reaction (see glossary)
- Blood flow is reduced to the gut, significantly reducing absorption of fluids and blood sugar (the brain's fuel)
- Normal repair/replacement of cells is supended
- Stress stimulates hormone secretions that quickly change emotions to a negative orientation
- We are not motivated to continue at a high level of performance
- Under repeated stressful workouts, competitive runners get sick. The protection mode shuts blood flow to the immune system, opening the door to infections.

1. You can train your body-mind for the stress in each area by using the program in the "Mental Training Program" chapter, page 29.
2. Do a reality check on the goal to make sure it is not too demanding, page 34.
3. Adjust speed sessions and do the workload while reducing the stress (rest interval adjustments, etc.).
4. Read the section in the glossary on TMS and prepare to deal with it.
5. Some mental training can be paired with workouts.
6. Reduce mechanical stress by using the ankle, see page 96.
7. Do what works for you.

Managing Unresolved Issues

When a person has experienced chronic pain or lingering depression, there are often unresolved subconscious stress issues, stimulating the reflex brain to reduce blood flow to areas that are damaged. Dr Sarno has an in-depth discussion of this in *The Mind-body Prescription.* His insight and advice have been very helpful for those with these issues, and I recommend this book highly.

- The problem does not have to be resolved, but it must be acknowledged.
- Internal rage from childhood issues is a common cause.
- Complex interpersonal issues are included in this category: Issues after a divorce, having to follow orders from a boss that one does not respect, and concern for parents or children that seem unresolvable.

Vent! At the beginning of a run, express your anger or rage. Shout if necessary; argue with the absent adversary; get in a good anger release. Then get on with the run. When you take conscious mental action, the executive brain in the frontal lobe takes control away from the reflex brain. With the conscious brain in charge, there is less chance that the subconscious will cause problems during the run. The natural calming effect of the run, with endorphins, will also shift production to positive motivation hormones/peptides.

7   Mental Training
Taking control by programming yourself for success

One of the first questions my wife Barbara asked me when I told her I was writing a book on motivation was "for what do you want to be motivated?" For most runners this seems easy to answer, at first: to finsh a long run in the upright position, to run faster at a given distance, to finish ahead of a sister, neighbor, age group competitor, to qualify for Boston, or my favorite, to enjoy my run.

But as you have discovered in the earlier sections of this book, the major challenge in maintaining motivation is that of diffusing stress while retaining the enhanced meaning in life that one feels from a run. The two are directly connected. A successful mental training program will reduce stress to a manageable level so that almost every run can bring joy and personal empowerment. The stage is then set for planning a realistic approach to your goal

Current attitude and beliefs determine which form of peptide is produced and what type of emotion is transmitted to the receptor cells, and the entire body-mind network. A positive attitude and belief in what you are doing will stimulate positive peptides. But an environment of too much stress for the individual will trigger negative emotions, with negative messages like "I'm too busy to run," "I'll get too tired," "It's not my day," or "Why am I doing this?"

In the previous chapter, several strategies are offered for diffusing stress. By taking conscious action, you can shift control away from the subconscious reflex brain. Dr. Lipton explains the power of the conscious components of the frontal lobe:

"Endowed with the ability to be self-reflective, the self-conscious mind is extremely powerful. It can observe any programmed behavior we are engaged in, evaluate the behavior and consciously decide to change the program. We can actively choose how to respond to most environmental signals and whether we even want to respond at all. The conscious mind's capacity to override the subconscious mind's preprogrammed behaviors in the foundation of free will." [10]

So by acknowledging the stress, diffusing it, and continuing to produce positive peptides through gentle running, you have started the process. The next step is to set up an ongoing mental training program that will "run you through" the anticipated challenges each day through a series of do-able steps. This will desensitize you to the negative messages while giving you a plan to succeed for that day or the season. The more you repeat the plan, the more you will reprogram the reflex brain. This improves your sense of belief in the system, which will stimulate positive attitude hormones.

The three elements of training that I've found successful for thousands I've coached are explained below. You can do the mental training during a run, while driving, during a quiet time in the morning or evening, or whenever works for you.

Early morning mental training can get you focused for that day. Going through the plan in the evening can consolidate issues from the day and prepare you for action the next day.

Each of the training modes presented will involve the conscious brain and empower the creative/intuitive right brain. For top performance, you will need to access both, and the training can mold them into a balanced team.

Even with a plan, workout or race stress will continue to result in negative attitude peptide production. So it is natural to receive doubts even during a workout that is hard but going well. Your conscious action to insert an extra walk break and desensitize yourself to negative messages will help you stay in the positive or neutral peptide zone.

Maintaining control over stress is important throughout each workout and during the training program journey. Most of the workout stress can be controlled by using the tools in the "Diffusing Running Stress" section of the previous chapter. Continue to explore ways of dealing with your individual issues.

When the stress is too high, right brain activity is reduced or shut off and you'll lose the creative problem solving and connections to inner resources. Adjusting to a slightly more conservative run-walk-run strategy will help to keep stress in balance better than any single adjustment I have found. For example, if you have been running for 3 minutes and walking for one minute, try a few rotations of 2-1 (or better, 1-1) to "catch up."

Desensitizing You will get to know the adversities of performance or endurance during the long runs and/or speed workouts. Write down the doubts and negative messages that you have received. Rehearse these and write down a response to each one. This maintains cognative control. For example, when you get the message "This is not your day", respond by saying "I can do it, I am doing it, I feel strong!"

Aches and pains – See the TMS section in the Glossary, and in the "Situations" chapter. It is important to know when you have really damaged something or are just under the influence of TMS. Don't hesitate to consult a doctor who wants you to continue running. He or she can help to draw the line.

Continuous increase in fatigue is a reality on long workouts. You can run with significant fatigue as long as you are within the guidelines of pacing and run-walk-run ratios.

Low blood sugar level will increase stress, negative peptides and reduce mental focus. Candace Pert, PhD, notes that blood glucose supports the ability of the neurons to store and secrete all of the messenger chemicals – neurotransmitters and neuro-peptides. So lower BSL means lower transmissions.[11] Eating a blood sugar booster is a simple fix. See the chapter on this topic in this book.

So let's now move on to the mental training techniques that can desensitize you to the stress buildup and prepare you to keep going at a realistic pace when it's really tough. Whether you are just trying to get out the door to run three days a week or pushing through strenuous speed training for a Boston Marathon qualifier, the principles are the same.

But we need a plan if we want to maximize our potential. We're rewarded by having more happy and life-enhancing moments when we do so. With a plan, you'll have more control over attitude, energy level, mental focus and life itself. The sustaining rewards come from finding out a bit more about who you are, choosing goals that are realistic and finding that you have more strength inside during challenges than you gave yourself credit for.

---

10 Bruce Lipton, PhD, *Biology Of Belief,* p. 103
11 Candace Pert, PhD, *Molecules of Emotion.*

8 Your Motivation Training Plan

Yes, you can train your mind to be motivated, just as you train your body to run farther or faster. Just having a plan that you believe in sets up a positive mental environment. Focusing on one small (and do-able) step at a time, you reduce stress significantly. By moving from one step to the next, you maintain mental momentum and take control over your motivation and training. As you do this pattern over and over, you reprogram the reflex brain so that the process becomes easier and easier. Here are the major concepts:

1. Do a reality check on your goal. Make sure that it is within your current capabilities and that you have enough time to perform the key workouts, while resting in-between. Keep evaluating your goals and adjust as you head toward the key dates on your calendar. This maintains conscious control over the process.

2. Acknowledge that the reflex brain responds to stress by sending negative messages to lower our motivation. Under severe stress, the reflex brain will reduce blood flow to the gut, frontal lobe and damaged areas to create pain and lower blood sugar level. Start talking to the reflex brain when this starts to happen, laugh, and tell it to open up the blood flow. This keeps you under conscious control.

3. Diffuse the stress by using one or more of the simple methods in the "Situations" chaper in this book. Keep telling the reflex brain that you know what it is doing, and that you will not let this happen.

4. Move forward by walking. Even if you are not going to run immediately, walk around the room thinking through the next steps in the "Jump Start" program below. Use the mantras that help you shift gears. The conscious shift to positive thoughts can change your mood in a few minutes by triggering the release of positive peptides.

5. When it is time for your run, go through the "Jump Start" program below. The endorphins you release will lock into receiver molecules all over the body, transmitting messages that you feel good, and you can do it.

6. During the run, or during other quiet periods (driving in a car, waiting for a flight or a meeting, etc.), identify the challenges you want to manage or overcome. List the negative messages you receive and the problems from past experiences. Then rehearse yourself through each situation.

7. Concentrate on one challenge at a time. Several common ones are presented in the "Situations" chapter, with success strategies.

8. Break up the challenge into a series of small steps that take you from the beginning of the first hints of the challenge to the successful finish. You can use the "situation" formats, amending them to your challenge, or use the format for personal issues.

9. Mentally rehearse the steps during various quiet periods of your day. Even if you don't know the solution to problems that come up, rehearse yourself digging down and getting through it, and finishing with a great feeling of accomplishment.

10. As you repeat the rehearsal, and fine tune it, you are reprogramming the reflex brain to automatically move from one step to the next when confronted with the challenge. It will then tend to set up an almost automatic series of steps.

11. As long as you experience the challenge, continue the regular rehearsal, adjusting to your situation, making it better and better.

A Reality Check On Your Goal
(Fill in the blanks and do the math so see if you are ready for your goal)

Goal Distance: _____

Goal Time: _____

Magic Mile Time: _____

Add 33 seconds for 5K pace: _____

Multiply by 1.15 for 10K pace: _____

Multiply by 1.2 for half marathon pace: _____

Multiply by 1.3 for marathon pace: _____

Add 2 min to the marathon pace prediction
for long run pace: _____

I understand that the pace predictions are based on perfect conditions and my doing all of the training in the time goal progam.

Agree _____

I understand that on the first race at any distance, a long run training pace is recommended for the first three quarters of the distance on race day.

Agree _____

Note: Training pace is at least 2 minutes per mile slower than the prediction made by the magic mile.

Jump Start Your Motivation

Almost every runner feels better after almost every run. But there are "those days" every year when the subconscious reflex brain is under a higher level of stress/pressure and will divert you away from thoughts about taking a run by sending messages like "there's too much to do." By taking conscious action, you can override the relex brain, feel better and get moving. Each of the simple actions below can improve mental attitude in each workout. Each of these actions stimulate the secretion of the positive attitude hormones that make you feel better physically and emotionally. As you take one step after another, you will gradually increase the flow of the "good attitude" substances and gain control over your attitude. Soon you will have confidence in the system, and it becomes easier and easier to get going.

- Eat a blood sugar boosting snack if needed – low blood sugar is a major stress on the brain. A simple snack of about 100 calories can often change attitude in 20-30 minutes. Some runners have had a rebound by taking a sip or two of a sugar beverage and spitting it out.
- Drink a cup of coffee, if you drink coffee and have no problems doing so. Caffeine is a central nervous system stimulant and helps with focus. Even one cup of coffee has been shown to increase endurance time on a treadmill.
- Start walking – The gentle motion of walking will stimulate good secretions of peptides, improving mood and motivation.
- Smile – Smiles not only activate endorphins, but stimulate positive peptides that lock into molecules and result in good emotions.
- Breathe in cadence with your steps – Rhythmical breathing has been shown to reduce stress and improve attitude. Take a lower lung breath every 3rd or 4th breath.
- Believe that you will feel better, and that you are doing something positive for yourself. Your positive belief in what you are doing activates positive peptides.
- Lower the adversity of the workout/race – If you are feeling stress/pressure when considering a pace of 9 min/mi, run 10 min/mi. If a 3-1 ratio seems challenging, use a 1-1. Shorter running segments often leave you feeling so strong that you increase speed at the end or at least "feel strong" at the end.
- See the "situations" section of this book for plans to get out the door on a low motivation day.
- Mantras – Talk to yourself. Use these or create your own.

I'm moving – I feel good
I know I can do this
I'm feeling better
The positive peptides are being received – I feel better
I'm changing my attitude
My exertion is making me feel better
One more minute
30 more seconds
10 more seconds
One more step, one more step, one more step

(See more in the "Mantras" chapter of this book.)

9   No More Excuses

All of us have days when we don't feel like exercising. Occasionally, you may need a day off due to sickness or too much physical activity. But usually this is not the case. Blame your excuses on the reflex brain, which is feeling stress and wants to reduce the possibility of more stress. Perceived workout stress triggers dozens of negative reflex thoughts about why we shouldn't work out. They are all perfectly logical and accurate. Believing in these messages will stimulate negative attitude peptides. But we don't have to believe them. Once you quickly decide whether there is a medical reason for these blasts, you'll usually conclude that the reflex brain is just trying to make you lazy.

Thinking ahead and organizing your day will reduce or eliminate most of these excuses. This activates the conscious brain, which shifts control away from the "reflex." You'll find pockets of time, more energy, quality time with kids, and more enjoyment in the exertion. You'll tend to be more productive in everything you do because you have "your time to yourself."

The following is a list of excuses that most of us hear on a regular basis. With each, there's a strategy for blasting them away. Most of the time, it's as simple as just getting out there. Remember, you can be the captain of your ship. If you take charge over your schedule and attitude, you will shift control away from the reflex brain, increase the flow of positive peptides and improve motivation to exercise. As you set up motions for dealing with each excuse, you can rewire the reflex brain into patterns that get you out the door.

As you move away from each excuse, turn the words in a positive direction and start moving:

"One foot in front of the other."

"The endorphins are flowing."

"The excuses are melting away."

"Life is good!"

"This _____ hurts!"

Most of us have several "weak links." These areas of the body are the first to hurt when we are stressed and talk to us more on the days when we have more stress. If there is no inflammation, loss of function, or real pain, it is usually OK to exercise. Indeed, exercise releases the stress that can erase or reduce the pains as endorphins are secreted to kill the pain. But if you have any medical concerns, talk to a doctor who wants you to keep exercising.

It's a physiological fact that stress can greatly aggravate the symptoms of your weak links. Read the TMS sections in the Glossary and in the "Situations" chapter in this book. You'll find more information about this in *The Mind-body Prescription* by Dr. John Sarno. While there is almost always some aggravation in an area of pain, stress can trigger the reflex brain to reduce the blood supply and aggravate the nerve response, producing an increase in the intensity of the symptoms. Gentle exercise can bring blood flow to the area while it releases stress. As you will see in the "Situations" segment, you can reduce or stop this TMS problem by shifting control to the conscious brain.

"I don't have time to exercise"

Most of the recent U.S. presidents have been regular exercisers, as well as most of their vice presidents. Are you more busy than the president? You don't have to exercise for 30 minutes straight. You will get the same benefit from your weekday workouts by doing them in pockets of time: 5 minutes here, 10 minutes there. Many who start an exercise program find that they don't need as much sleep as they get in better shape, and exercising for 30 minutes or so gets the day started. It all gets down to the question "Are you going to take control over the organization of your day or not?" Spend a few minutes in the morning to arrange your schedule. By making time for exercise, you'll also tend to be more productive and efficient, and will "pay back" the time. The bottom line is that you have the time – seize it and you will have more quality in your life. Your loved ones will appreciate this too, because after a workout, you're nicer to them.

Tip: Cramped for time? Just walk or run for 5 minutes

The main reason that runners don't make progress is that they don't exercise regularly. Whatever it takes to keep you going every other day do it. Even if you only have 5-10 minutes, you will maintain most of the adaptations. Besides, if you start with the idea of going out for 5 minutes, you'll usually stay out for 10 or 15.

"People will talk about me"

Many people deprive themselves of the fat-burning, vitality enhancement and attitude boost of walking or running because they are afraid that someone driving by will see them exercising and judge them in some way. Actually, most people admire and respect those who spend the energy to exercise, whether they look like athletes or not. Besides, it's not a good idea to let the opinions of unknown people stop you from doing something that can enhance your life.

"Exercise makes me tired"

If this happens, you are the one responsible. You have almost complete control over this situation. By starting each walk or run with a good blood sugar level, paced conservatively, with sufficient "shuffle" or walk breaks, you can feel better and more energized than before you started. If you have a bad habit of going too fast in the beginning, then get control over yourself! As you learn to slow down, you'll go farther and have more energy at the end and afterward. Be sure to have a snack within 30 minutes of finishing the run: 100-300 calories. It's best to have 80% of the calories from simple carbohydrate and 20% from protein.

"I don't have the right build (or technique) for exercise"

Just go to any big marathon and you'll see an amazing diversity of body types – including those who weigh more than 300 pounds. Virtually every one of us is genetically designed to walk or run, and when we do so regularly, our movements become more and more efficient and natural. Even if you don't have smooth form, you can enjoy the way you feel during and afterward. With all of the different pieces of equipment, you can find one that will work for you.

"I need to spend some time with my kids"

There are a number of exercise strollers that allow parents to walk or run with their kids. My wife Barbara and I logged thousands of miles with our first child, Brennan, in a single "baby jogger." We got a twin carrier after Westin was born. With the right pacing, you can talk to the kids about anything, and they can't run or crawl away.

You can also run/walk around a playground as you watch them play, or run around a track while they play on the infield. Home equipment allows busy moms and dads to get in their workout as they watch kids napping or watching TV, or talk with them while they are playing.

"I've got too much work to do"

There will always be work to do. Several surveys have found that exercisers get more work done on days they work out. A good run (when paced correctly) can leave you with more energy and a better attitude while you prepare to manage your day. All of this comes with an erasure of stress. Hundreds of morning exercisers have told me that during the quiet morning exercise, they plan their day and solve problems. Others say that the after-work "workout" relieved stress, tied up some of the mental loose ends from the office, and allowed for a transition to home life. You will get as much (probably more) work done each day if you work out regularly.

"I don't have the energy to exercise today"

This is one of the easier ones to solve. Most of the exercisers who've consulted me about this excuse had not been eating enough times a day. I don't mean eating more food. In most cases, the quantity of food is reduced. By eating about every 2-3 hours, most feel energized, more of the time. Even if you aren't eating well during the day, you can overcome low blood sugar by having a "booster" snack about an hour before a workout. Caffeine, taken about an hour before exercise, helps (as long as you don't have caffeine sensitivities). The dynamic food duo that I use is an energy bar and a cup of coffee. Just carry some convenient food with you at all times.

"I don't have my running shoes and clothes with me"

Load an old bag or backpack with a pair of running shoes, a top for both winter and summer, shorts and warmup pants, towel, deodorant, baby wipes, and anything else you would need for exercise and clean up. Put the bag next to the front door or in the trunk of your car, etc. Then the next time you are waiting to pick up your child from soccer, etc., you can do a quick change in the restroom and make some loops around the field, school, etc.

Primary Causes of Low Motivation

- Time goals are the primary reward from running
- Goals are unrealistic at present
- Not enough rest between stress workouts
- Running too hard most running days
- Not enough "joy runs" each week
- Not enough walk breaks in long runs and sometimes other runs
- Running with a group that is too fast for you
- Feeling sorry for yourself because you have no support
- No consistent plan
- The training plan used is too stressful for you

10 Mental Training Programs

"You can gain control over your attitude, your performance and your pain."

- Training programs can reprogram the reflex brain
- You have the power to take charge over motivation and improve attitude
- Rehearsal drills break up a task into do-able steps, performed step-by-step
- Magic words tap into successful patterns and our intuitive/creative powers
- Dirty tricks will distract your reflex brain, not activate the frontal lobe
- How to manage/eliminate pain's hold over your motivation

The choice is yours. You can take control over your attitude, or you can let your reflex brain go through a series of negative reactions that usually result in low motivation and reduced performance. By using the proven strategies in this chapter, you can turn a negative attitude into a positive one, reprogram the reflex brain to stay on track toward a positive goal, and tap into the incredible powers of the right brain. Whether you struggle to get out the door when running by yourself, or you need more motivation to keep going when it's tough, you have a better chance of success when you have a strategy. This is your motivational training program.

To understand motivation, look inside the mental command and response center. The center of action, especially when under physical challenges, is the subconscious reflex brain. When stress accumulates to a significant level, this powerful center takes protection action to reduce motivation and reduce effort level.

A stream of messages is released telling us to "slow down," "stop and you'll feel better," "this isn't your day," and even philosophical messages like "why are you doing this?" Stress secretions of peptides lock into molecules all over the body transmitting an emotional environment that is unmotivated and negative. Reflex brain also reduces blood flow to the frontal cortex and to areas of damage that it has already identified. This results in a sensation of pain that normally would not be due to the damage alone. This pain is the result of TMS (tension myositis syndrome).

Note: I am not suggesting that you should run through pain when there is chance of a serious injury. When you have pain in a weak link area that you suspect is an injury, check with your doctor to verify. In many cases, the pain is stress-induced TMS and can be managed.

By engaging the conscious brain in the frontal lobe, you can usually stay on track and very possibly push to a higher level of performance even when there is significant stress. See the "Confronting TMS" section in the "Situations" Chapter.

The first step is to go through the stress diffusion proceedure in the "Why Do We Feel Unmotivated" chapter 6. Then you are ready to go through a series of mental training drills that will reprogram your reflex brain. With the conscious brain always in charge, you can back off the effort if there is a legitimate issue of health or safety (very rare), or check your "magic mile" to ensure that your goal is not out of your current range of ability.

These drills can allow you to move from one do-able step to the next. By managing pace and diffusing stress, the creative and intuitive right side of the brain can be active and search for solutions to current problems with connections to your inner resources – your spirit.

Drill 1
Rehearsing Success

Rehearsal has been used for decades by individuals in various fields to achieve their potential on any given day, under a variety of conditions. Mentally envisioning a series of challenges and rewards, all the way to the goal, gears up the mind-body team to work together at top capacity.

1. Rehearsing realistic fatigue, aches and pains, negative messages, doubts, etc., desensitizes one to the challenges.
2. A series of small steps. The conscious frontal lobe reprograms the reflex brain to stay focused by breaking down a challenge into segments, one leading automatically to the next to the successful finish.
3. As the rehearsal is repeated and fine tuned, the reflex brain can be reprogrammed to move you from one step to the next, instead of responding to the negative motivation reflex due to stress/pressure.

Rehearsal drills are listed in the "Situations" chapter, with step-by-step formats. These are a good starting point for most runners but need to be adapted to the individual. The principles are as follows:

What: This is a mental storyline of how you want the experience to unfold. At first, you may focus on specific parts of a workout or race that have been challenging for you. You may continue to rehearse only the challenging parts or tie the parts into a continuous preview of the whole experience. Most runners "fast forward" through the less challenging segments and focus on the "issues" that have caused problems. An experienced rehearser will move though a marathon rehearsal within 2-3 minutes at the end of a season.

When: Rehearsals can be done during a run, when driving, in the shower, waiting for a flight, etc. Trying out the rehearsal during a hard workout can help you fine tune it to be more effective. Many go through key rehearsal segments during long runs.

Be realistic and positive: The effectiveness of this mental drill will depend upon your being honest about the real challenges, rehearsing through them, making adjustments, digging down, but always getting though with pride, satisfaction and a great sense of accomplishment.

Desensitize: Revisit the negative messages that have come up or physical challenges that could happen during the event. As you visualize getting through these, you desensitize yourself to surprises that could add stress during the event.

Rehearse the problem: (even if you don't know the solution): By envisioning a past problem that you haven't solved, including your "digging down" and getting through it, you empower the creative/intuitive right brain to find solutions. It often does this by race day (without telling you because it is subconscious).

A series of small steps: Challenges are not confronted head-on, but segmented into do-able units. So when there is a significant hill that you are worried about, you visualize shortening the run segments, shortening stride length, accomplishing one segment at a time, and not focusing on the top of the hill until you are congratulating yourself for moving over the top, smoothly gliding down the other side.

Each segment leads automatically to the next: By rehearsing the segments attached to one another, you are more likely to move from one to the next when you get into the challenge.

Rehearse a variety of weather conditions, aches and pains, etc..: As you envision a variety of possible challenges, you will not only be better prepared for what could happen, but you are training the various body-mind components to work as a team to get the job done.

Finish with a vision of success/accomplishment: Always rehearse success that is realistic. Yes, you feel tired, but you crossed the finish with strength and dignity.

Note: The actual rehearsal drills are in the "Situations" section, a few pages from now. Be sure to read the inspirational stories in the "Inspiring Stories" chapter.

Drill 2
Magic Words

Even the most motivated person has periods during a tough workout or race when he or she wants to abandon the goal. By using a successful brainwashing technique, you can use the resources from past successes to pull yourself through these negative thoughts and feel like a champion at the end. Associate these successes with key words, and you can build on this success and confidence with each use.

Think back to the problems that you face in your tough workouts or races. These are the ones that are most likely to challenge you again. As you go through a series of speed sessions and long runs, you will confront just about every problem you will face. Go back in your memory bank and pull out instances when you started to lose motivation due to these, but finished and overcame the challenge.

My Three Magic Words: Relax ... Power ... Glide

In really tough runs, I have three challenges that occur over and over: 1) I become tense when I get really tired, worried that I will struggle badly at the end; 2) I feel the loss of the bounce and strength I had at the beginning, and worry that there will be no strength later; 3) My form starts to get ragged, and I worry about further deterioration of muscles and tendons and more fatigue due to "wobbling."

The problems themselves are almost never serious. The key word is "worry." When you focus on the negative possibilities, you stimulate negative hormones and build anxiety. This adds stress to the reflex brain, which will trigger more negative attitude peptides. So by focusing on problems, you will lose motivation.

My big motivational breakthrough was learning to counter these three problems with the magic words "Relax...Power.... Glide." The visualization of each of these positives shifts mental control to the conscious frontal lobe of the brain. The real magic comes from the association I have made with hundreds of successful experiences when I started to "lose it" in one of the three areas but overcame the problems. Each time I "run through" one or more of the challenges, I associate the experience with these magic words and add to the magic. Positive peptides are released, attitude improves, stress is released, and confidence improves.

Now, when something starts to go wrong, I repeat the three words over and over. Instead of increasing my anxiety, the repetition of the words calms me down (negative hormones are neutralized). Even though I don't feel as strong in the last mile as I did in the first one, I'm empowered just by knowing that I have a strategy and can draw upon my past experience (more positive attitude hormones are secreted). And when my legs lose the efficient path and bounce, the right brain is empowered to take over and make adjustments, finding the inner strength to go on, as it has in past successes.

When I say magic words that are associated with successful experience there are three positive effects. The saying of the words floods the brain with positive memories. For a while, the negative messages of the left brain don't have a chance, and you can get down the course for a half mile or more. But the second effect may be more powerful. The words directly link you to the right brain, which works intuitively to make the same connections that allowed you solve the problems before. Finally, the saying of positive workds stimulate positive hormones which change your attitude for the better.

To be successful on any day, you must first finish the race. Most of the time you can get through the "bad parts" by not giving up and simply putting one foot in front of the other. As you push beyond the negative left brain messages, you create the confidence to do this again and again. Each time you use the magic words and feel the results, you are reprogramming the reflex brain. Feel free to use my magic words or develop your own. The more experiences you have associated with the words, the more magic.

Drill 3
Playing Dirty Tricks on the Reflex Brain

The strategy of the rehearsal drill will get you focused, organized, while reducing the stress for the first third to half of the race or workout. Magic words will pull you along through most of the remaining challenging sessions. But on the really rough days, it helps to have some dirty tricks to play on the reflex brain.

These are quick fixes that distract the reflex brain's "garbage" messages for a while, allowing you to keep going for the next segment of the course. These imaginative (and sometimes crazy) images don't have to have any logic behind them. But when you counter a left brain message with a creative idea, you can confuse the left brain and stop the flow of negative messages.

Even more important is the shift that occurs in peptides and the right brain. The conscious action of an image, as mentioned below, will shift action to the frontal lobe where you can take command. This can change the peptides from negative to positive. Having fun with these visualizations will unlock more positive hormones, improving confidence and attitude.

A shift to creative images can further shift action to the right brain. This often triggers a series of creative thoughts that can entertain you. Once engaged, the right brain can subconsciously solve problems, dig into your inner resolve to keep going, find hidden strength, etc.

The Giant Invisible Rubber Band

When I get tired at the end of a hard race, I unpack this secret weapon and throw it around someone ahead of me or someone who had the audacity to pass me. For a while, the person doesn't realize that he or she has been "looped" and continues to push onward while I get the benefit of being pulled along. After a minute or two of mentally projecting myself into this image, I have to laugh for believing in such a absurd notion. When you take charge over the situation by projecting an set of behaviors and acting on them, you activate the conscious brain to take control. Furthermore, laughing activates the creative/resourceful right side of the brain. This usually generates several more entertaining ideas, especially when you do this on a regular basis.

The right brain has millions of dirty and entertaining tricks. Once you get it rolling, you're likely to receive intuitive solutions to current problems. It can entertain you as you get closer to your finish, step-by-step. Most important, this circuit can empower the legs, feet and muscles to do what they are capable of doing on that day. The result will often surprise you.

More dirty tricks:

- A jet engine behind you

  When you start to slow down, imagine that there is a jet engine from a giant 777 aircraft blasting you from behind – run in this tailwind

- Oxygen molecules in your shirt

  When you are feeling the fatigue from a hard run, tap your shirt 3 times and inhale. There are powerful oxygen molecules released that will help to revive your muscles

- Bouncy air pads on your feet

  During the last third of your race, when you feel that the feet aren't bouncing any more, turn on the mental switch that inserts air into the skin on the bottom of your feet. It is only activated if you shorten stride and keep your feet low to the ground

11 Situations

Rehearsing Success & Programming the Reflex Brain

Rehearsals develop patterns of thinking and motion that retrain the reflex brain to move from one small step to the next. If you mentally rehearse these often enough, you will get into a "groove" to do the behaviors you need to do. In a challenging situation, you don't want to have to think about the stress or challenge. If you have rehearsed a plan of action enough times, you can move from one step to the next almost automatically. The power of the rehearsal is that the conscious brain can format the reflex brain for a series of actions so that you don't have to think. By repeating the pattern, you'll revise it for real life and become the successful runner you want to be!

Getting Out the Door Early in the Morning

The most common motivational problem, as presented to me by runners over the last three decades, is how to get out of bed early enough and be ready to do a long run, hard workout, race, or simply a run that was assigned for that day.

State your desired outcome: To be awake and fully engaged in the run, from the start.

Detail the challenge: Desire to lie in bed, no desire to exert yourself so early. The stress of the alarm clock and having to think about what to do next when the brain isn't working very fast.

Break up the challenge into a series of actions, that will lead you through the mental barriers, no one of which is challenging to the left brain.

1. The night before, lay out your running clothes and shoes (often near the coffee machine) so that you don't have to think.
2. Set your alarm, and as you are laying in bed, say to yourself over and over: Alarm off.....feet on floor....to the kitchen. Or, simply stated:

   Alarm....feet....kitchen

   As you repeat this, visualize doing each action without thinking. By repeating it, you lull yourself to sleep. You have also been programming yourself to take action the next morning.

3. The alarm goes off. You shut it off, put your feet on the floor, and head to the kitchen all without thinking because you programmed the reflex brain to do this.

4. You're putting on one piece of clothing at a time, sipping coffee (tea, diet cola, etc.), never thinking about exercise.

5. With coffee cup in hand, clothes on, you stick your head out the door to see what the weather is like.

6. Driving to the workout or race, sipping your beverage, you rehearse seeing friends, feeling the positive energy of an event, easing into the workout/race, feeling good about your exertion.

7. Or, you walk to the edge of your property, put the coffee cup down, and cross the street. You're on your way.

8. The endorphins are kicking in. The positive peptides are rising, you feel good, you want to continue.

Principle of lazy physics: A body in the bed wants to stay in the bed. But once a body is in motion, it wants to stay in motion.

Getting Out the Door
After Work, School, a Tough Day

Many runners must run in the afternoon but commonly feel drained at the end of the day. This is another instance of the reflex brain responding to the stress of the day, often due to low blood sugar, which triggers negative peptides that leave you feeling tired and unmotivated.

State your desired outcome: To get out the door and be running down the road.

Detail the challenge: Stress-induced negative mood hormones that result in a negative attitude. Desire to sit on the couch or take a nap. The thought of a workout is stressful which can trigger more negative secretions and negative messages.

Reduce stress as you are driving or walking home by saying "I'm going to get home, put on some comfortable clothes and eat and drink." This reduces stress in several ways. There is no thought given to running, and even the thought of eating and drinking can stimulate positive peptides.

1. Put on some comfortable clothes and shoes – they just happen to be running attire.
2. Eat an energy snack (easily digestible) and drink water or a caffeinated beverage (if OK with you). Caffeine can shift mood very effectively.
3. Think relaxing thoughts
4. Stick your head out the door to check the weather.
5. Walk around outside to see what's going on.
6. Cross the street and you're on your way.

Principle of lazy physics: A body on the couch wants to stay on the couch. But once a body is in motion, it wants to stay in motion.

Break up the challenge into a series of actions, which lead you through the mental barriers, no one of which is challenging to the left brain.

Finishing a Tough Workout

You're into a hard workout, and you are really tired. By focusing on the negative thoughts, the negative attitude peptides transmit their messages into the receptors, leading to less motivation. This triggers messages such as "This isn't your day," or "You can't reach your goal today," or "Just slow down a little," "There are other days to work hard," or "Do this workout again when you are more motivated."

Evaluate whether there is a real medical reason why you can't run as projected. If there is a reason, back off and conserve – there will be another day.

Almost every time, however, the problem is more simple: you are not willing to push through the discomfort. *You are letting your reflex brain keep you from your goal.* To do your best in a race, you must learn how to deal with these problems in workouts. As you push through the motivational slumps, you will develop the internal resources to do so when you have even more challenges later. You will also change the chemistry inside the muscle cells.

Focus on the next segment of the workout. If you have one mile left, tell your conscious brain that you are going to run a quarter of a mile. As you start to run at a pace that is OK, and you are focusing on a distance you know you can finsh, positive hormones are produced, and your attitude shift begins. Passing one quarter mile, you agree to do another quarter of a mile, and congratulate yourself for moving forward. Segment by segment you get through the mile and feel good about completing it. More positve secretions push your mood to the positive and keep the negative emotions away.

Say positive things: "I'm pushing back my barriers," "I'm overcoming challenges," "This is making me tougher." As you add to the number of repetitions each workout and talk to the frontal lobe, you allow it to reprogram the reflex brain and lock into a series of steps to get through the fatigue at the end of the workout. By the time you run the goal race, the reflex brain is ready to click in to one positive step at a time to get to the end.

Confront left brain messages with strength statements: Don't quit! I can do it!
Mental toughness starts with, simply, not giving up. Just ignore the negative messages, stay focused on the next few steps, and talk to yourself. This shifts control to the frontal lobe and away from the reflex brain. Positve affirmations activate positve peptides.

I Can Do the Next Segment

Champions feel the same discomfort, they just hang on longer and get through it.

In your speed workouts, practice the following drill. Fine tune this so that when you run your goal race, you will have a strategy for staying mentally tough with a flood of positive peptides.

The scene:
You're getting very tired, you'd really like to call it quits, or at least slow down significantly.

Quick strategies
- Break up the remaining workout into segments that you know you can do.
- "1 more minute" – Run for one minute, then reduce pace slightly for a few seconds, then say "1 more minute" again and again.
- "10 more steps" – Run about 10 steps, take a couple of easy steps, then say "ten more steps."
- "One more step" – Keep saying this over and over – you'll get there.

Take some gliding breaks

- Reduce the tension on your leg muscles and feet by gliding for a few strides every 1-2 minutes. The acceleration-glider drill prepares you for this moment, particularly when coasting downhill.
- As you say "I'm gliding...I'm running smoothly," you continue the mental shift to the positive.

Segment by segment

- If you really question your ability to get through the workout, start each repetition, or race segment, saying to yourself just one more" (even if you have 4 to go) or "10 more steps." "I'm getting it done!"
- Teamwork! If you are on a team, or have made a communication pact with a friend, you can pull motivation from the other person or persons. Think about your team members, say to yoursel, "I feel your strength." The perception of team bonding can pull you through many difficult workouts and shift your additude hormones in your favor.
- When you are getting close to the end and really feel like you can't keep going, say to yourself "I am tough" or "I can endure" or "Yes, I can" or "One more step."
- Smile!

Finishing a Tough Race

At any stage of a hard race, even in the first third, you can encounter problems that bring doubt and trigger negative messages from the reflex brain. If you focus on these messages, you will produce negative attitude peptides.

- By rehearsing every negative message you could receive, you will desensitize yourself to their attitude-lowering effect.

- Confront each negative with a positive statement.

The negative is ...	**The positive is ...**
"Back off, this isn't your day."	"Don't give up!"
"There are other races."	"I can do it"
"Why are you doing this?"	"I'm getting tougher!"

- Evaluate whether there is a real medical reason (which is rare). If there is a health problem, back off and conserve – there will be another day.

Most commonly, the reflex brain is responding to the stress buildup of the the race by triggering negative peptides, creating a negative emotional environment. A successful strategy during the first onset of this attitude downturn is to glide a little. If needed, take a short walk break (15-20 seconds) to mentally regroup and focus on the next segment of the race.

- Activate your rhythmic breathing (mentioned in the in the "Jumpstart Your Motivation" section, page 35. Smile and start running again with a light touch and smooth cadence. Each one of these actions engages the frontal lobe and stimulates the positive peptides to transmit a message of hope throughout the body.

- To do your best in a race, you must manage the stress buildup by using a routine such as those that follow. You are training yourself to keep going, which is 90% of the battle. You are also programming the conscious brain to regularly check on the reflex brain, stop the negative thoughts and insert positive beliefs.

Note: None of these drills is cast in stone. Adapt them to your needs and strengths. You will continue to edit them as you move through the process.

- Continue to confront left brain messages with strength statements: Don't quit! I can do it!

In your speed workouts, practice the following drill. Fine tune this so that when you run your goal race, you will have a strategy for staying mentally focused and positive. Your belief in a plan will increase the production of positive motivational hormones.

The scene:
You're getting very tired and stressed in a race, and you'd really like to call it quits or at least slow down significantly.

Quick strategies
- Break up the remaining race into segments that you know you can do.
- "1 more minute" – Run for one minute, then reduce pace slightly for a few seconds, then say "1 more minute" again and again (or 30 seconds, or 15 seconds, etc.).

- "10 more steps" – Run about 10 steps, take a couple of easy steps, then say "ten more steps."
- "One more step" – Keep saying this over and over – you'll get there.

Take an extra walk break to "gather yourself" if you need it.

Take some gliding breaks. By doing the "acceleration-glider" drill, you will be prepared to do this in the race.

- Reduce the tension in your leg muscles and feet by gliding for a few strides every 1-2 minutes. The acceleration-glider drill prepares you for this moment, particularly when coasting downhill.

Segment by segment

- In the workouts, if you really question your ability to finish, start each repetition, or race segment, saying to yourself, "just one more" (even if you have 4 to go) or " 10 more steps." You'll make it the whole way.

- Teamwork! You are needed by the team. Belonging to a larger group with team spirit can pull you through many difficult workouts. Even if you only have a long distance friend who you are going to report to, it helps to have that connection. Some runners bring their cell phone on long runs and call their friend as a "lifeline."

- When you are getting close to the end and really feel like you can't keep going, say to yourself, "I am tough" or "I can endure" or "Yes, I can" or "One more step."

"I can do it....I am doing it...I did it!

Coming Back from an Injury

If there has been damage that has kept you from running, make sure that the area has healed enough to start walking. Get clearance from a doctor who wants you to get back into running as soon as you can. When given permission, start with a 10-minute walk and always walk or run with a relatively short stride, feet low to the ground. Every other day, extend the walk by 3-5 minutes until you reach 30 minutes. Then insert a 10-second jog, every minute, into your walk. If this is too much for you at first, walk the second half of the workout. Take the day off from running after a day you have inserted the running segments into your walk. You can walk on the "off" day if you are not having problems walking.

Your goal is to finish each run/walk feeling like you could continue for another 10 minutes or more without any huffing and puffing or any pain from weak links. When you feel comfortable at 10 sec run/50 sec walk for 30 minutes, on one day a week (usually the weekend) extend the time by 5 minutes, every other weekend until you reach an hour. On the shorter weekend, stay at 30-40 minutes. Shift to doing two other runs a week (usually Tues/Thurs) and increase the amount of running. When 10/50 feels "too easy" on the shorter runs, move up to 15/45. After 3-6 of these workouts, shift to 20/40. You could either stay at one of those strategies or continue to gradually increase (as long as there is no huffing and puffing) to 30-30, then 1-1, then 2-1.

Remember that your muscles, heart, blood system, and mind-body connections can all work as a team if you progress gradually and avoid setbacks. If you have any aches and pains or lingering fatigue, drop back to a more comfortable ratio and treat the area if there is possible damage. Tell your doctor about any medical issues that could indicate issues from your injury.

Read the last "situation" in this section (on TMS) if you have pains. In most cases, pain generated by TMS can be managed while you continue to train. Always consult a doctor who wants you to continue to run if you suspect there is significant damage that requires a layoff. Stay below the threshold of irritation when there is damage.

Don't allow your reflex brain to send negative messages, like "You used to be in such great shape" or "This is baby stuff, you can push yourself today" or "You'll never get back to your former fitness level."

Instead, talk back to the reflex brain to shift control to the frontal lobe.
"I'm getting back in shape."
"I feel good about myself."
"I have overcome an injury and am a smarter runner now."
"Speed is not important – it's the joy from each run that keeps me going!"

- Put a date on a calendar – your mission is to finish a 5K/10K/half or full marathon.
- Make a commitment to join a group that runs at your ability level.
- Get a friend to stay in touch with you as you get in shape. Email, text and call one another when needed.
- Say to yourself when the motivation starts to lower, "I can do it, I can do it!"
- Believe in yourself.

Positive affirmations at the start of a downturn can get positive peptides locking into receptor molecules, sending positive messages toward an emotional comeback.

Note: See the positve mantra section in this book.

Coming Back from an Illness

Don't run if you have a lung infection. A virus in the lungs can move into the heart and cause serious damage. When there is a significant infection, get clearance from a doctor who wants you to get back into running as soon as you can. When permission is given, start with a 10-minute walk and always walk or run with a relatively short stride, feet low to the ground. Every other day, extend the walk by 3-5 minutes until you reach 30 minutes. Then insert a 10-second jog every minute into your walk. If this is too much for you at first, walk continuously when needed. Don't do any running the day after you have inserted running segments into your walk in order to rest the running muscles.

Your goal is to finish each run/walk feeling like you could continue for another 10 minutes or more without any huffing and puffing. When you feel comfortable at 10 sec run/50 sec walk for 30 minutes, on one day a week (usually the weekend) extend the time by 5 minutes, every other weekend until you reach an hour. On the shorter weekend, stay at 30-40 minutes. Shift to doing two other runs a week (usually Tues/Thurs) and increase the amount of running. When 10/50 feels "too easy" on the shorter runs, move up to 15/45. After 3-6 of these workouts, shift to 20/40. You could either stay at one of those strategies or continue to gradually increase (as long as there is no huffing and puffing) to 30-30, then 1-1, then 2-1.

Note: Don't feel compelled to move up and up. Find a ratio that works and feels comfortable.

There are a lot of issues in coming back from an illness. Even when you feel somewhat normal living a sedentary life, the body may not have repaired itself completely. Remember that your muscles, heart, blood system, and mind-body connections can all work as a team if you progress gradually and avoid setbacks. If you have any aches and pains or lingering fatigue, drop back to a more comfortable ratio and treat the area if there is possible damage. If you suspect that there are medical issues concerning your recovery from the illness, check with your doctor.

Read the last "situation" in this section (on TMS) if you have pains. In most cases, pain generated by TMS can be managed while you continue to train. You may need to get your doctor to evaluate whether there is damage in the area that could be increased by running. Stay below the threshold of irritation of a real damaged area.

Don't allow your reflex brain to send negative messages, like "You used to be in such great shape" or "This is baby stuff, you can push yourself today" or "You'll never get back to your former fitness level."

Instead, talk back to the reflex brain:
"I'm getting back in shape!"
"I feel good about myself!"
"I have overcome an illness and am making a smart comeback now."
"Speed is not important – it's the joy from each run that keeps me going!"

- Put a date on a calendar – your mission is to finish a 5K/10K/half or full marathon if the body allows.
- Make a commitment to join a group that runs at your ability level. Get a friend to stay in touch with you as you get in shape. Email, text and call one another when needed.
- Say to yourself when the motivation starts to lower, "I can do it, I can do it!"
- Believe in yourself.
- When you reach a motivational lull, walk for 5 minutes. In most cases, after a short walk, you will run-walk-run for at least 30 minutes. But even if you walk only, you can help to turn the emotions around by producing positive hormones.

Positive affirmations at the start of a downturn can get positive peptides locking into receptor molecules, sending positive messages for an emotional comeback.

Coming Back from an Extended Layoff

If you have not run for two weeks or more, assume that you have lost all of your conditioning. The good news is that you can regain the fitness you had, in less time that it took originally by conservatively increasing your running according to the plan below. If there are medical issues, get clearance from a doctor who wants to help you return to running as soon as you can. When there are no issues, start with a 10-15 minute walk and always walk or run with a relatively short stride, feet low to the ground. Every other day, extend the walk by 3-5 minutes until you reach 30 minutes. Then insert a 10-second jog every minute into your walk. If this is too much for you at first, walk continuously when needed. Don't do any running every other day in order to rest the running muscles.

Your goal is to finish each run/walk feeling like you could continue for another 10 minutes or more, without any huffing and puffing. When you feel comfortable at 10 sec run/50 sec walk for 30 minutes, on one day a week (usually the weekend) and extend the time by 5 minutes, every other weekend until you reach an hour. On the shorter weekend, stay at 30-40 minutes. Shift to doing two other runs a week (usually Tues/Thurs) and increase the amount of running. When 10/50 feels "too easy" on the shorter runs, move up to 15/45. After 3-6 of these workouts, shift to 20/40. You could either stay at one of those strategies or continue to gradually increase (as long as there is no huffing and puffing) to 30-30, then 1-1, then 2-1.

There are a lot of individual issues in coming back from an extended layoff. Above all, find some joy in every run. Don't push too far beyond current limits. Remember that your muscles, heart, blood system, and mind-body connections can all work as a team if you progress gradually and avoid setbacks. If you have any aches and pains or lingering fatigue, drop back to a more comfortable ratio and treat the area if there is possible damage. If you suspect that there are medical issues during your comeback, check with your doctor.

Read the last "situation" in this section (on TMS) if you have pains. In most cases, pain generated by TMS can be managed while you continue to train. You may need to get your doctor to evaluate whether there is damage in the area that could be increased by running. Stay below the threshold of irritation of a real damaged area. Most of these aches are temporary and are not cause for alarm.

Don't allow your reflex brain to send you negative messages, like "You used to be in such great shape" or "This is baby stuff, you can push yourself today" or "You'll never get back to your former fitness level."

Instead, talk back to the reflex brain:

"I'm getting back in shape!"

"I feel good about myself!"

"Speed is not important – it's the joy from each run that keeps me going!"

- Put a date on a calendar – your mission is to finish a 5K/10K/half or full marathon if the body allows.
- Make a commitment to join a group that runs at your ability level. Get a friend to stay in touch with you as you get in shape. Email, text and call one another when needed.
- Say to yourself when the motivation starts to lower, "I can do it, I can do it!"
- Believe in yourself.

Positive affirmations at the start of a downturn can get positive peptides locking into receptor molecules, sending positive messages toward an emotional comeback.

Coming Back After a Bad Race or Workout

All runners have bad days. The most prominent factor that sets a champion apart from others is the ability to move forward after a setback. Spend a few minutes trying to learn what you may have done that brought on the problem and you will improve in many ways. Read the "Troubleshooting" section at the end of this book for solutions to common problems.

A bad run will trigger negative messages, such as "You are losing it" "Running isn't fun anymore" You'll never get to your goal," "Why are you doing this?" If you focus on these and believe them, you will allow the reflex brain to create negative beliefs, stimulate negative peptides and lower your motivation. Here are some steps for turning your attitude in a positive direction

1. Reestablish the joy of running. Take several easy runs with enough walk breaks to leave you feeling good from the beginning. Don't set time goals for these runs. The positive hormones will start the shift to a good attitude.
2. Ignore negative messages. They will flow into your brain; let them flow out.
3. List the mistakes or causes of the bad run.
4. If there is a significant issue that is unresolved (specific mistakes made by you or others), deal with it at the beginning of the run. Vent and get this frustration/rage/anger out of your system –let it go.
5. State one positive aspect of the problem run.
6. Come up with a plan to avoid this happening again.
7. Believe in the plan.

Burning More Fat

It is possible to burn fat without running 100 miles a week or being hungry all the time. The secret: staying focused on running and walking, and monitoring food intake.

There are many pleasurable hormones received from eating. In *The End Of Overeating*, David Kessler, MD, explains how eating various combinations of sugar, salt and fat trigger the neurotransmitter dopamine into delivering various degrees of drug-like pleasure. Comfort food experiences that are often repeated become hardwired into the reflex brain as a stimulus-response activity. So when we are talking to friends at a party with a bowl of potato chips nearby, it is common to subconsciously eat one after another, without being aware of doing so. The taste of each is so rewarding that we can't stop at one....or 20.

Concepts of fat burning

- Aerobic running burns fat. Liberal walk breaks help you stay aerobic.
- Long, aerobic runs can adapt the muscle cells to be better fat burners.
- During speed training and fast running, you're not burning fat but glycogen (stored form of carbohydrate). Slower is better for fat burning.
- Walking is aerobic – the more steps you take, the more fat you burn without a significant hunger response.
- Monitor food intake by using a program or website that tracks this.

Tools that can help you shift away from the reflex brain

1. Use a website like www.fitday.com to monitor intake and analyze nutrition.
2. Use a resource like *A Woman's Guide to Fatburning* by Barbara and Jeff Galloway for backup information and to understand the process.
3. Set your calorie deficit goal each day (150 is the maximum recommended).
4. Set up a calorie "budget" for each day.
5. Get a step counter and increase the number of walking steps to achieve your calorie deficit (10,000 is the goal).
6. As you monitor your eating and exercise, you gain control and can take action to improve efficiency of the process. You control your budget.
7. By increasing walking steps to 10,000, you can eat a few more calories and still lose fat.

How to modify reflex eating behaviors

- Estimate calorie content before eating anything – this shifts consciousness to frontal lobe.
- If there are foods that you really love, which are hazardous to your diet, eat small amounts.
- Search for foods that are healthy that you can gradually swap for the hazard foods.
- Reward yourself for making progress with non-food items.

A Close Running Friend Moves Away, etc.

The loss of a faithful running companion is stressful and results in lower motivation to run. When a running dog dies, for example, many runners lose motivation and cut themselves off from the good peptides that could turn their attitude around.

If the person moves away, call him/her on the cell before a run. Talking and hearing the voice can recharge many of the positive motivational peptides that can get you out the door. Many runners actually bring a cell phone with them and call when the motivation runs low. Some call this their "lifeline" or "motivation connection."

Go to races, talk to other runners in your neighborhood, attend running club meetings. Look for running groups, like the Galloway programs. Most runners who reach out for another running buddy find one.

Stay in touch with your friend and run together in a race (mutually agreed upon). This is very common and keeps the positive attitude peptides transmitting good messages.

Managing TMS

Dr. John Sarno is an orthopedist who practiced traditional medicine for years. Then he discovered a condition called tension myositis syndrome (TMS) and developed methods of treating it. This dramatically improved his cure rate. I recommend his books *Mind-Body Prescription* and *Healing Back Pain* because they have helped thousands of people manage or eliminate chronic pain and get on with their lives.

As the runner starts a workout, it helps to identify sources of stress and talk them out or just vent as you're moving down the road. Dr. Sarno says that you don't have to resolve an issue to manage or cure the pain, you just need to be aware of it and then take some conscious action to move control away from the reflex brain.

Sarno explains how inner stress buildup activates TMS. The reflex brain receives continuous information flow through the peptide network, which identifies the areas of the body that have been damaged.

When total stress level rises significantly for the individual, the unconscious reflex brain reduces blood flow to these areas, dramatically increasing pain. But when patients take conscious control over the reflex brain by deciding to do things like talk to the reflex brain, the blood flow can be restored and there can be a reprogramming of the reflex brain.

"I know what you are doing, reflex brain, and I won't allow it."
"Open up the flow in my_____."
"I'm in control here!"
"I'm not going to let the reflex brain control the blood flow."

Note: Before running, when there is pain, get guidance from your doctor to ensure that some running/walking will not make the condition worse. It's best to be under the care of a doctor who understands TMS and wants you to run if you can.

Reprogramming the Reflex Brain to Use Run-Walk-Run

Most children have been instructed in physical education class or on a sports team to "never walk." A common coaching statement that is embedded in the reflex brain is "walking is failure." There are reasons why coaches will instruct their students to keep running during short events. But it is not necessary to follow this advice for the rest of our lives.

It's a fact that this childhood programming is very powerful. When we start to take a walk break, even 20 years after we finished our last cross country race or PE class, stress builds up in the reflex brain and anxiety hormones are produced. The reflex brain may also trigger your memory to remind you what your coach said (or at least a fuzzy remembrance).

But there's hope. We can reprogram the reflex brain to accept taking walk breaks as normal. Here's how:

1. Use the magic mile to determine a realistic goal pace and a conservative long run pace.
2. Set the run-walk-run ratio based upon the pace per mile of both the goal pace and the long run pace, using the "Galloway Run-Walk-Run" chaper in this book.

3. Read the chapter and load yourself up with all the key phrases. Memorize these or write them down so that you can talk back to the reflex brain's negative messages:

- Walk breaks make me strong – to the end
- Walk breaks allow me to do what I want to the rest of the day
- Walk breaks speed my recovery
- Walk breaks help me run faster
- Walk breaks let me control fatigue
- Walk breaks break up the distance into do-able segments
- Walk breaks give me control over my running enjoyment

4. Get a run-walk-run timer or program your watch for segments. A $20 timer is available on our website and will get you into a rhythmical pattern of run-walk-run. This is a great way to reprogram the reflex brain.
5. At the end of each run, make a conscious statement about how the run-walk-run method is superior to your old way. "I have a tool to enjoy running for life."

You are the one who determines how much you run and how much you walk

One of the wonderful aspects of running is that there is no definition of a "runner" that you must live up to. There are also no rules that you must follow as you do your daily run. You are the captain of your running ship, and it is you who determines how far, how fast, how much you will run, walk, etc. While you will hear many opinions on this, running has always been a freestyle type of activity in which each individual is empowered to mix and match the many variables and come out with the running experience that he or she chooses. Walk breaks can keep the first-time runner away from injury and burnout, and can help veterans to improve their time.

12 The Final Countdown

Rehearsing the goal race is the most effective mental preparation I've found for runners who are approaching a race that challenges them. As you get closer to the deadline on race day, you will sense more stress. Most of the runners I've worked with in this area have noticed some phantom aches and pains during this period that were not felt before or after. Using the drill in the TMS section of the last chapter will help you understand the process.

As you practice each of these routines before long runs, you will feel more and more confident when you approach race day. Here is a plan that you can customize for your needs and the logistics of your race.

The Afternoon Before

Some like to run a little and some don't run at all the day before the race. You won't lose any conditioning if you take two days off from running leading up to the race. This is a personal issue and the number of days you do not run before a race is your choice. If you run, think positive thoughts. Say "I am ready" and "I can do it."

The carbo loading dinner

Some events have a dinner the night before. At the dinner, you can talk with friends, family members and other runners. Don't over-eat! Many runners assume, mistakenly, that they must eat a lot of food the night before. This is actually counterproductive. It generally takes at least 36 hours (usually longer) for the food you eat to be processed and useable in a race. It is very unlikely that you will get any significant nutritional help from the "last supper" before the race. Too much "loading" can lead to "unloading" during the event.

The Day Before

While you don't want to starve yourself the afternoon and evening before, the best strategy is to eat small meals or snacks that you know are easy for the body to digest. Taper down the amount as you get closer to bedtime. As always, it's best to have done a "rehearsal" of eating so that you know what works, how much, when to stop eating, and what foods to avoid. Work on your eating plan the evening before each long run, come up with a successful menu, and replicate as you approach raceday.

Drinking

The day before, drink 8 glasses (8 oz) of fluid, spread throughout the day, with two of these glasses being a sports drink. Don't drink a lot of fluid during the morning of the race itself. This can lead to bathroom breaks during the race. Many races have porto-johns around the start area, but some do not. This is another reason to preview the venue – noting the locations of bathrooms.

Tip: As soon as you awaken, drink a glass of water or a cup of coffee and don't drink until the start of the race.

The Night Before

For those who have had digestive problems during other races, Eating is optional after 5pm. If you are hungry, have a light snack that you have tested before and has not caused problems. Less is better, but don't go to bed with a low blood sugar level. Some can continue to consume small amounts of water or electrolyte beverages (4-6 oz) within the 3 hours before going to bed and some cannot. Avoid alcohol and salty food. Drinking alcohol the night before competition can reduce performance potential. The effects of this central nervous system depressant carry over to the next morning. Alcohol is also a dehydrating agent.

Sleeping

Don't worry if you don't sleep much or at all before your big race. Many runners every year tell me that they run their best times after sleep-deprived nights. Don't keep yourself up on purpose, but if it happens, don't worry about it. It is the worry that stimulates negative attitude hormones, not the lack of sleep.

Pack your bag and lay out your clothes so that you don't have to think very much on race morning.

Pack:
- Your watch
- Your run-walk-run timer set for your raceday strategy
- A pace chart, or wrist band, with split times, or mile times
- Shoes (with the finish chip attached, if used)
- Socks
- Shorts
- Top – see clothing thermometer
- Outer garment in case of precipitation. Many use a garbage bag with a "head hole"
- Pin race number on the front of the garment in which you will be finishing
- Bring along a few extra safety pins for your race number (bib number)

- Water, sports drink (such as Accelerade), pre-race and post race beverages (such as Endurox R4), and a cooler if you wish
- Food for the drive home
- Bandages, skin lubricant, any other first aid items you may need
- Cash for post-race celebration meal
- A few inspirational thoughts, jokes or stories to provide laughs or entertainment before the start
- Team garments, etc.

Race Morning

Drink 6-8 oz of fluid upon waking. In most cases, this is out of the system before the start. There will be no nutritional benefit from eating breakfast, but some runners do it for "comfort." Diabetics should follow the advice of their nutritional consultant. Above all, follow the program that has worked for you before long runs.

Race Day Checklist

Photocopy this list so that you will not only have a plan, but you can carry it out in a methodical way. Pack the list in your race bag. Don't try anything new the day of your race except in the case of health or safety issues. Stick with your successful plan.

Fluid and potty stops – after you wake up, drink 6-8 oz of water, 2-3 hours before the start (or use the plan that has worked for you). In order to avoid bathroom stops, stop your fluid intake according to your timetable.

Eat – what you have eaten before your harder runs. Don't try anything new and avoid problem foods. It is OK not to eat at all before a race unless you have specific issues (such as diabetes), in which case you should go with the plan that you and your doctor/nutritionist have worked out.

Get your bearings – walk around the site to find where you want to line up and how you will get to the start.

Start your warm up 20-30 min before the start. You may only walk to get the legs moving, but please, move those legs for at at least 10 minutes of very gentle motion. If possible, go backwards on the course and preview the start and finish segments for about half a mile each and turn around. This will give you a preview of the most important parts of your race – start and finish. Use the warm up ritual that has worked for you in past workouts and races. Here is a standard one:

- Walk for 5-10 minutes, slowly *this may be the only warmup for non time goal runners*, who may use the first two miles as their gentle warmup.
- Jog slowly for 10 minutes.
- Over the next 15-18 minutes, jog over the start and the finish areas. Visualize starting and finishing.
- Walk around for 3-4 minutes.
- *Time goal runners:* Do 4-8 acceleration-gliders that gradually increase to the speed you will be running in the race.
- Get in position and focus on the side of the road where you want to go for your walk breaks
- When runners are called to the start, talk and joke with others. Relax.

Note: Practice this warmup before one workout every week to get your routine set.

After the Start
Remember that you can control how you feel at the end by being conservative in the beginning.
- Stay with your plan. Take every walk break for the first half of the race at least. If the reflex brain gets anxious as runners pass you, smile and say, "I'll see you folks later." You will!
- Believe in yourself; say, "This is my proven strategy for a strong finish."
- Even if you are pushing fairly hard, enjoy the race as much as possible, smile often.
- On warm days, pour water over your head at the start, possibly wetting your running top.

After Mid-Race
- When the going gets tough, do everything you can to relax and keep the muscles resilient.
- Keep going – don't give up. Shorten your stride and increase turnover – especially going uphill.
- During the last half mile, don't let your legs slow down. One more step! Success is not letting up. You can do it!

At the Finish

- Your finish is important – you are part of a team of positive runners
- Keep a quick rhythm – even when very tired
- Stay in the upright position
- Cross the finish with a smile on your face
- You did it!

After the Finish

- Keep walking for at least a quarter of a mile
- Drink about 4-8 oz of fluid
- Within 30 min of the finish, have a snack (100-300 calories) composed of 80% simple carbohydrate/20% protein (Endurox R4 is best) *if this is not available, choose a simple carbohydrate snack.*
- If you can soak your legs in cool water during the first two hours after the race, do so (cool water, faucet water – ice is not necessary)
- Walk or jog for 20-30 minutes later in the day
- Celebrate with friends and family!

The Next Day

- Walk for 30-60 minutes, very easy. This can be done at one time, or in installments.
- Keep drinking about 4-6 oz an hour of water or sports drink.
- Write down what you would do differently in your next race.

13 Inspirational Stories

Billy Mills

The person who inspired me most grew up on the Pine Ridge Native American Reservation in South Dakota. Billy was selected to attend a boarding school where he discovered that he could run faster than other boys in the distance events. Realizing that this could be his path to success in life, he worked very hard and won a scholarship to the University of Kansas.

Billy has a positive sprit and envisioned himself becoming one of the best distance runners in the NCAA. This did not happen. He came to believe that his best events were longer ones and set his sights on the 10,000 meter. His coach, however, wanted him to run shorter events, and lots of them. The training prescribed on the university team did not prepare him for his 10K event, and he did not achieve what he thought was possible during the 4 years in Lawrence, KS.

Post-graduate running programs were few in 1961, but Billy found one: The US Marines. After his officer training, he was assigned to the team at Quantico, VA, setting his sights on the Olympic 10K. His times were not yet good enough to qualify for the US Olympic Trials, but he felt strongly that he would improve and qualify. Progress was slow.

A college running friend of Billy's returned to his native country after graduation (Australia) and trained with the 10K world record holder at the time, Ron Clark. Every week for about 3 years, Billy would get his "intelligence report" detailing Clark's workouts. Billy tried them and was usually unsuccessful. But at the end of the hard portion of his workout, Mills envisioned that Clark was just ahead of him, so he shifted into his best finish "kick" and would imagine himself zooming by the world record holder, breaking the tape and becoming the Olympic champion. Almost every day for 3 years, this fantasy world was enacted.

In 1963, I went to watch the National Cross Country championships in New York City with some college friends. At the meet, I looked up an alumnus of my school, Wesleyan University, who was Officer in Charge of the Marine Team. When he discovered that I might be interested in applying in a few years and that I was interested in the 10K, he introduced me to Billy.

I instantly liked Billy. I didn't understand it at the time, but there was something about his attitude that impressed me. Later, I came to understand that he had a subtle confidence that I had not encountered before. Mills was probably ranked about 25th going into that race. Without bragging, he told me that he was going to finish near the top. He did.

I followed Billy in *Track & Field News* as he continued to improve, qualified for the Olympic Trials and then, unexpectedly, made the team in the 10K and the marathon. That experience made a major imprint on me. If Billy could come out of obscurity and make the Olympic Team, maybe there was hope for me.

Billy Mills was not our best 10K runner (Lindgren) and was not ranked very high among the entrants in the 1964 Tokyo Olympic 10K. But somehow he sensed that he had a chance to win. There was no trial heat, only a final with over 60 athletes running 25 times around the track.

The excitement and focus drove Mills to push the pace and, at halfway, he realized that he had run only one second slower than his fastest 5K. He was feeling the overexertion and feared that he had spent his resources. He looked for a place to drop out. Just before he stepped off the track, he glanced into the stands and happened to focus on one person – his wife Pat.

He couldn't drop out with her watching, believing in his dream, so he decided to just finish the race. This released the pressure to win. Several runners passed him and then a group of about four went by. Something intuitively told Billy that he should go with that group and he did. Ron Clark was in the group.

Billy admits that he doesn't remember very much about the last four laps. He was running on instinct, trying to put one foot in front of the other, hoping not to fall. The group passed one runner after another and as they approached the "bell lap" (one to go). Billy was in lane 2, with Ron Clark in lane 1. They were approaching a slower runner who was a full lap behind, and Clark tapped Billy's arm, trying to get him to move out so that both could pass the runner. Billy was so "out of it" that he didn't know he was bring nudged. So Clark finally shoved Billy out into the 4th lane and passed the runner.

The third member of the group, Mohammed Gamudi from Tunisia, was right behind, saw the altercation and took off after Clark. His arms were swinging erratically as he passed Mills and the sharp part of his elbow hit Billy very hard in his upper arm, hitting a nerve. The pain was great enough to wake Billy up and the reflex brain sent a primitive message from his playground days: When someone whomps you, you whomp them back. But his slow-twitch endurance muscle cells were spent, and he could not respond. The front two runners moved away from Billy and were about 30 meters ahead as Billy rounded the curve and looked at the finish only 100 meters away.

Billy was living the situation that he had rehearsed almost every day for three years. Without thinking, he did what he had programmed himself to do. And because he had practiced sprinting at the end of his hard workouts, he had trained his fast-twitch muscle fibers to respond.

Mills zoomed by Gamudi and Clark, broke the tape and became the Olympic champion. This is the greatest come-from-behind victory in the history of the Olympic 10K.

Racing Cancer

"If I had to choose between my old pre-cancer life as a somewhat depressed, overweight, unmotivated and unfulfilled couch potato and my current life with cancer, it's easy. I'm energetic, happy, motivated and love life each day." – Lee Kilpack

In 1996, Lee Kilpack was diagnosed with breast cancer, with lymph node involvement. She began a treatment plan of surgery, chemo, and radiation. Lee had never exercised. The diagnosis was a shock to her spirt, and the treatment tested body, mind and will power.

By 2000, things weren't looking too good, and she felt bad most of the time. Then, one morning, she woke up with the desire to start taking care of her body. She hired a personal trainer that day. By 2001, she was walking every day. Later that year she had inserted some running into the walks. In 2002, Lee walked the 3-day, 60-mile Breast Cancer Walk and raised $3,000 for the cause.

The training for and competion of such a strenuous event resulted in a big letdown in motivation, with extended recovery from injuries, aches and pains. Lee struggled and finally started running regularly in December 2003. After the '04 New Year, Lee set a bigger goal – to finish a marathon in November. The training program she chose was too advanced and she became injured in September. She didn't give up.

In early 2005, her doctor cleared Lee to start running again. She picked up my conservative training program after attending our Blue Mountain beach retreat. worked with her via email and often found it hard to hold back her energy and drive.

The training for the Marine Corps Marathon was more of a challenge than for most because she relocated to the Gulf coast to volunteer for relief efforts after Hurricane Katrina, squeezing in runs after exhausting days. Somehow, she also hikes, cycles, and paddles hard in her kayak; on the "off days" she doesn't run.

She regularly gets screened for tumor markers. While the tests show her out of the normal range, her doctor does not see a threat in the near future and supports her running.

"I don't know what the future holds for me. If it is metastasis tomorrow, I would be OK with that. What a good life I've been given. My health and happiness have never been better. What my oncologist doesn't understand is what a dynamite combo vitality and endorphins make."

Marathon Records After Age 80

Mavis Lindgren was a sickly child and sickly adult who was advised against exercising. She almost died of a lung infection in her late 50's. During the recovery, her new young doctor had the shocking opinion that she should walk with her husband and kept recommending an increase in the distance she covered.

Surprisingly, Mavis found enjoyment as she felt her body come alive with improved endurance. In her 60's, she took up running with husband Carl and quickly surpassed him. Into her late 80's, she was setting age group records and had not even suffered a common cold since beginning her running career.

At about the age of 85, she slipped on a cup at the 20-mile water station at the Portland, OR, marathon. Officials helped her up and tried to take her to a medical tent. She quietly brushed them off, saying that it was a surface injury. After she finished, however, she went to the medical tent to find that she had been running with a broken arm.

Dave Wottle: Don't Give Up

Because he was very thin and feeble, the Wottle family doctor recommended exercise, especially running. Dave felt at home on the track team. Like many distance and middle distance runners, however, he had to work hard to see modest improvements in junior high and high school track. At Bowling Green

State University, he improved significantly every year and moved to the top of the NCAA rankings. He was at his performance peak during the 1972 US Olympic trials.

While the commentators were expecting running legend Jim Ryun to win the US trials 1500 meters, Dave won easily. He also had no problem winning the 800 meter. During a workout the week after the trials, Dave injured his knee. Three weeks later, when we reported for our Olympic tour, Dave was still injured and had not been able to train.

The coaches wanted to send him home and bring in a healthy runner. Dave refused. Reluctantly, the coaches supported Wottle. By working with the athletic trainers and the medical team, he was able to run, and he gradually regained some conditioning.

After the gun fired on his first 800 meter heat in Munich, Dave was at the back of the pack. He struggled to move up as he rounded the final turn, passing one runner, then another. At the finsh, he leaned, finished third and was the last qualifier for the next round.

Due to conditioning issues, Dave ran a similar race in the next two qualifying heats, coming from behind to barely qualify for the finals.

In the final, the competitors clumped together, going for the gold. Unfortunately, Dave could not keep up and had fallen about 30 yards behind at the halfway mark. Many competitors would have stepped off the track. But Dave set his sights on the next-to-last competitor and caught up with him as they rounded the final curve.

Two runners bumped one another and Dave darted between them. He ran inside to pass three more and outside to pass another group. As he approached the finish, there was a line of the leaders ahead and, at the last minute, a parting occurred. Dave dove through, broke the tape and won the gold medal.

TV announcers were amazed at his finish spurt, but this was not the case. His 200 meter splits were almost identical. Dave knew what he could do and stuck with his plan.

At any given point, logic showed that Dave Wottle should have given up his spot and let someone else run. Dave won because he did not give up.

85 Pounds Lighter – Inspired by a Training Group

Tracy B added the usual weight during her pregnancy and then continued to add more afterward – almost 100 pounds over "healthy weight." One day, she decided to take small steps, literally, by walking in her neighborhood. Then, she found a charity marathon team that motivated her to take the next step. "The marathon team became a part of me, like a little extension of my family." Instead of restricting her diet, Tracy exercised portion control and eliminated high-fat snacks. Each step reinforced her positive lifestyle as the pounds were burned off during exercise. The best part, according to Tracy, was that she entered a new and wonderful world of exercise.

Lasse Viren – When You Get Knocked Down, Get Up

During the Munich Olympics, the star performer in my event, the 10,000 was not well known going into the games. Unlike most athletes who move onto the world class scene over a 4-8 year period, Lasse's times were not spectacular. When I checked on his performances the year before the Olympics, I noted that he had finished 17th in the European Championships 10K.

Lasse's joy was running through the wilds, mile after mile. He loved forest trails and had a variety of routes and workouts. About the only time that you saw Lasse on a track was during a race. But as Lasse ran his trails, he would envision being in the big race, responding to various challenges and coming back strong.

In the trial heat of the 10,000, Lasse ran a smart race and qualified easily without seeming to be very tired. None of the experts I spoke with before the 10K final predicted that he would finish in the top 5.

The 10K final evolved into a strategic race. With about 8 laps to go (out of 25) there were 10 runners tightly bunched, all in position to win the race. With no warning, Lasse was tripped by a runner and he fell into the infield of the track, rolling over.

The first action that impressed me was that Lasse ran straight back to where he had been tripped. If he had tried to run the tangent he would have taken too many steps on the infield and been disqualified. There was no doubt in my mind that he had rehearsed this possibility.

The second impressive action was not trying to catch up with the field in the first lap or two. Lasse gradually caught up with the pack over the next two laps but he didn't stop there. During the next two laps he passed one runner at a time.

With two laps to go, Lasse moved into the lead and continued pick up the pace every 20 yards or so. There were several runners near him with half a lap to go, but Lasse steadily moved away from them. He not only won the gold, but he set a world record.

Lasse won the 5K gold medal in Munich and returned to Montreal four years later to capture gold in the 5K & 10K and finish 5th in the marathon.

145 Pounds Lighter

"I have traded my addiction to food for an addiction to running, I truly believe running has allowed me to cope with the mental and physical stresses of daily life, motherhood, and work more effectively."

Angela was an overweight kid from an obese family. By the age of 35, she weighed 280 pounds and suffered high blood pressure and back, knee, and hip pain. She also had a serious gastric reflux problem, and surgery was recommended.

In January of 2005, after months of psychological counseling and exercise (primarily walking and elliptical), she had the gastric bypass operation. She soon discovered that surgery doesn't change a genetic predisposition to obesity, nor the desire to cope with stress by overeating (many patients gain back some of their weight after these surgeries). Because of her surgery, she had to eat less and avoid certain foods because of their physical side effects.

Having enjoyed the stress relief of the pre-operation exercise, Angela continued to walk. Six months later, and 85 pounds lighter, she decided to "step it up" by inserting some short running segments into her walks and completed a 10K, and then a half marathon during the training season. By this time, she had lost a total of 120 pounds, crediting running with "revving up" the fat burning.

Looking for some guidance, she joined our Galloway Training program, finished the Richmond Marathon and set her sights on the "original" marathon in Athens, Greece. Despite some health setbacks during training, she kept improving her endurance and lost another 25 pounds. On the difficult Greek course (with a 13-mile hill), Angela set a new personal record by 22 minutes!

Overcoming an Eating Disorder

Julie was an overweight child (190 lbs) who enjoyed horseback riding and Pop Tarts but had self-esteem issues. After breaking her foot from falling off a horse, she fell into depression and didn't eat much for several weeks. For the first time in her life she was receiving a lot of positive attention and let her weight drop to 110!

Calorie intake was so limited that she had no energy to walk or move around at all. Intuitively, she felt she needed to run, which triggered an appetite increase and a return to a healthy running weight of 145. She then came to college. Faced with a lot more activities and stress, she dropped running, using food for comfort. Her weight boomed up to over 200 lbs.

Feeling that she could not control her eating habits, Julie engaged in something she could control – running. She felt better about herself, started to lose weight, and trained for a half marathon. Unfortunately, she did not take walk breaks and burned out.

Love intervened as Julie and Chris trained for a marathon together. She discovered that the right portion of food, training, and rest intervals give her the weight and body composition she wants. And she can eat Reese's Peanut Butter Cups as part of her calorie budget.

14 Training Tools That Manage/ Lower Workout Stress

When workouts and rest are balanced, stress can be managed, reducing a build-up and overload that otherwise would trigger negative peptides, lowering motivation. When you find a way to insert joy into a run, even stressful workouts can leave one feeling positive. Too many hard workouts or challenges that exceed your current ability result in lingering fatigue and increased stress. This stimulates production of negative neuropeptides, which send their low motivation messages. If corrections are not made, the reflex brain will often reduce blood flow to weak links, the gut, muscles, and the frontal lobe, causing pain, loss of energy, reduced muscle function, and foggy mental focus.

Here are some proven ways to regain control over your attitude and motivation:

1. Set realistic goals each season. Use the "magic mile" explained in this book to set up a "leap of faith" goal. See pp. 83-86.

2. The body responds better to gradual improvement allowing the many internal systems to improve your infrastructure without being exhausted and/or breaking down. A 3% performance improvement is realistic during a training season, while a 5% improvement is possible but very challenging. See pp. 83-86.

3. A modest improvement of 3%, every 6 months, is more likely to lead to steady and progressive changes over several years.

4. Use the "magic mile" time trial in this book to monitor improvement – a reality check. See pp. 83-86.

5. The long runs are the most important training component in any training program. They will bestow the endurance necessary for your goal. You cannot go too slow on the long ones. I recommend running at least 2 minutes per mile slower than your "magic mile" is predicting in the marathon itself, but it is better to go at a pace that is 3-4 min/mi slower. For maximum benefit, build the series of long run distance runs beyond the distance of the race, as noted in the schedules in *5K/10K, Half Marathon, Marathon, Galloway Training Programs,* and *Year Round Plan.* By going farther than marathon distance, you may never "hit the wall" again.

6. Be sure to read the "Galloway Run-Walk-Run Method" chapter in this book. Go with the the ratio of running to walking, as noted. It is always OK to take walk breaks more frequently.

7. *Time goal runners:* On non-long-run weekends, run a series of speed workouts as noted in *year round plan, half marathon, marathon, galloway training programs,* etc. These train you to deal with the physical and psychological challenges during the last 6

miles of your race, where your time goal is either made or compromised. These push back your performance wall, both mentally and physically.

8. Insert sufficient rest between the stress workouts to allow all the body parts to rebuild. Rest is crucial if you want to benefit from the hard workouts instead of increasing the fatigue level or breaking down with injury. On low mileage days, even if you have a form drill or hill workout scheduled, if you feel that you need to jog easily on that day and shorten the mileage, do so.

9. Back off when your "gut instinct" tells you that you may be getting injured. The prime reason that runners don't achieve their goal is "injury interruption" with a loss of capacity. When your intuition tells you that you may have an injury and there are signs of this, stop the workout and take an extra day or two off. Consult with a doctor about medical issues.

10. Cadence drills can reduce mechanical stress by helping you run smoother and more efficiently. These are scheduled into short runs during the week (usually Tuesday and Thursday). See page 103.

11. The acceleration-gliders train the muscles to "shift gears" when needed so that you're ready for any challenge. They also help you glide to save muscle resources while maintaining speed. See pages 103-105.

12. Hills build just the right amount of strength to deal with hills on your race course. They also help you run more efficiently. See the "Hill" section, pages 107-109.

15 The "Magic Mile" Is Your Reality Check

A major source of stress is the choice of a goal that is unrealistic. Sadly, many runners don't know what is realistic. In the early 1990s, I started using a one-mile time trial (called a "magic mile" or MM) as a reality check on current time goals. After looking at the data from thousands of runners, I've found this to be the best way to predict the best performance possible during a training program. By adding 2 min./mile to the predicted marathon pace, one can set a conservative long run pace that will reduce injury risk. By the end of the training program, I've found the MM to be the best predictor of a potential top performance in an upcoming race.

This one tool gives you control over your goals and your pacing. Making regular "reality checks" on your current potential activates the frontal lobe, taking control over the anxieties that are generated by the reflex brain. Maintaining control and setting realistic goals activate the positive peptides, which improve attitude and motivation.

The "magic mile" time trials (MM) are reality checks on your goal. These should be done on the weeks noted on the schedule. The MM has been the best predictor of current potential and helps to set a realistic training pace. With this information, you can decide how hard to run during various situations. (If you have any injuries, you should not do the MM.)

- Warm up for the MM with about 10 minutes of very easy running with liberal walk breaks.
- Do 4-6 accelerations as in the book – no sprinting.
- Run around a track (or a very accurately measured segment) if at all possible.
- Time yourself for 4 laps (or an accurately measured mile). Start the watch at the beginning, and keep it running until you cross the finish of the 4th lap.
- On the first MM, don't run all-out: run at a pace that is only slightly faster than your current pace.
- Only one MM is done on each day it is assigned.
- On each successive MM (usually 2-3 weeks later), your mission is to beat the previous best time.
- Don't ever push so hard that you hurt your feet, knees, etc.
- Jog slowly for the rest of the distance assigned on that day, taking as many walk breaks as you wish.
- At the end of the program, do the math listed in the next section: "Galloway's Performance Predictor."
- Training pace is at least two minutes per mile slower than the predicted maximum marathon pace (MM x 1.3).

After you have run 3 of these MMs (not at one time, on different weekends) you'll see progress and will run them hard enough that you are huffing and puffing during the second half. For prediction purposes, you want to finish feeling like you couldn't go much farther at that pace. Try walking for about 10-15 seconds at the half during the MM. Some runners record a faster time when taking short breaks, and some go faster when running continuously. Do what works for you on the MM.

Galloway's Performance Predictor

Step 1: Run your "magic mile" time trial (MM) (4 laps around the track)

Step 2: Compute your mile pace for the marathon by multiplying by 1.3**
For the half marathon, multiply by 1.2
For the 10K, multiply by 1.15
For the 5K, add 33 seconds per mile

Example:
Magic mile time: 10:00
For the best possible marathon pace, currently, multiply 10 x 1.3 = 13 min per mile
For the fastest long run training pace, add 2 minutes per mile = 15 minutes per mile
(remember to slow down 30 sec/mile for every 5 degrees above 60F) It's always better to go slower on the long runs.

Current half marathon potential is 12 min/mi
Current 10K potential is 11.5 min/mi or 11:30
Current 5K potential is 10:33 per mile

In order to run the time in the race indicated by the MM:**
- You have done the training necessary for the goal: long runs, speed sessions, form drills, race rehearsals (see www.jeffgalloway.com)
- You are not injured
- You run with an even-paced effort
- The weather on goal race day is not adverse (below 60F or 14C, no strong headwinds, no heavy rain or snow, etc.)
- There are no crowds to run through or significant hills

The "Leap of Faith" Goal Prediction

I have no problem allowing my e-coach athletes, who've run one or more races at a given distance, to choose a goal time that is faster than that predicted by the MM at the beginning of a 6-month program. As you do the speed training, the long runs and your MMs, you should improve, but how much? In my experience, this "leap of faith" should not exceed 5%. More commonly, the speed-up is in the 3% range.

1. Run the MM time trial
2. Use the formula above to predict the pace you could run now, if you were in perfect shape for your race
3. Choose the amount of improvement during the training program (3-5%)
4. Subtract this improvement amount from 2 – this is your goal time

How much of a "leap of faith?"

Pre-racing season prediction (Over a 5-6 month training program)	* 3% improvement	* 5% improvement
7:00 per mile marathon pace	6:47	6:39
8:00 per mile pace	7:45	7:36
9:00 per mile pace	8:43	8:33
10:00 per mile pace	9:42	9:30
11:00 per mile pace	10:40	10.27

Finish Time Improvement Pre-season marathon or half prediction	3%	5%
3:00	2:54:36	2:51:00
3:30	3:23:42	3:20:00
4:00	3:52:48	3:48:00

The key to goal setting is keeping your ego in check and the goal pressure/stress reduced. From my experience, I have found that a 3% improvement is more realistic. This means that if your marathon or half marathon time is predicted to be 3:00, then it is realistic to assume you could lower it by five and a half minutes if you do the speed training and long runs as noted on my training schedules in this book. The maximum improvement, which is less likely, is a more aggressive 5% or 9 minutes off a three-hour marathon.

In both of these situations, however, everything must come together to produce the predicted result. Even runners who shoot for a 3% improvement and do all the training as described achieve their goal slightly more than 50% of the time during a racing season. The more aggressive performances usually result in success about 20% of the time. There are many factors that influence your finish time in a race that are outside of your control: weather, terrain, infection, etc. Because of all the variables on race day, it often takes 3-4 races during a season to achieve success. Don't give up!

"Magic Mile" Time Trials (MM's) Give You a Reality Check Throughout the Season

- Follow the same format as listed in the pre-test above.
- By doing this as noted, you will learn how to pace yourself.
- Hint: it's better to start a bit more slowly than you think you can run.
- Short walk breaks will be helpful for most runners.
- Note whether you are speeding up or slowing down at the end, and adjust in the next MM.
- If you are not making progress then look for reasons and take action.

Reasons why you may not be improving:

- You're over-trained, and tired. If so, reduce your training for a week and/or take an extra rest day.
- You may have chosen a goal that is too ambitious for your current ability – set a new goal.
- You may have missed some of your key workouts or too many of your maintenance runs.
- The temperature may have been above 60F (14C). Higher temperatures will slow you down (the longer the race, the more heat will influence the result).
- You ran the first lap or two too fast.

Final Reality Check

Take your fastest MM. **If the tests are predicting a time that is slower than the goal you've been training for, go with the time predicted by the "magic mile."** It is strongly recommended that you run the first one-third of your goal race a few seconds per mile slower than the pace predicted by the MM average.

Use a Journal!

Read the next chapter about using a journal. Your odds of reaching your goal increase greatly with this very important instrument. Psychologically, a journal empowers you to take responsibility for the fulfillment of your mission.

16 Your Journal Gives You Control Over the Training

Regular Journal Checks Can Reduce Stress

Following a schedule that you believe in will bestow confidence and reduce stress. Regularly seeing the results of your planned workouts energizes your beliefs, builds more confidence and produces more positive attitude peptides. Your mental interaction with the journal moves you out of the control of the reflex brain and bestows more control over the process.

This is your book

Yes, you are writing a book. You already have the outline: your weekly schedule in this book. As you follow it, your journal will document the good times and the slow ones. It will allow you to modify your plan and track the changes. Later, you can look back after success or disappointment and often find reasons for either. If we don't look back at the history of our setbacks, we will have a tendency to repeat them.

The various types of journals

- Calendar facing you on the wall

Many runners start recording their runs on a wall calendar or one that is posted on the refrigerator. Looking at the miles recorded is empowering. But equally motivating for many is the avoidance of too many "zeros" on days that should have been running days. If you're not sure whether you will really get into this journal process, you may find it easiest to start with a calendar.

- An organized running journal

When you use a product that is designed for running, you don't have to think to record the facts. The spaces on the page ask you for certain info, and you will learn to fill it very quickly. This leaves you time to use some of the open space for the creative thoughts and ideas that pop out during a run. Look at the various journals available and pick one that looks to be easier to use and carry with you. I've included a sample page of my Jeff Galloway Training Journal (available at www.JeffGalloway.com)

Week of **Jan 1**

Thursday
GOAL 35 min easy (sc)
TIME 45 min
DISTANCE @ 6.5
AM PULSE 49
WEATHER Cloudy
TEMP 40°
TIME 6 PM
TERRAIN rolling
DATE Jan 4
WALK BREAK —

COMMENTS
Great run with Barb, Wes + Sambo — who took out the pace too fast + died at the end. The rest of us caught up on the gossip. Achilles ached so I iced it for 15 minutes.

Friday
GOAL 45 min (sp) 5 x 800 meter
TIME 1:15
DISTANCE 7.5 mi
AM PULSE 53
WEATHER 45°
TEMP Sunny
TIME 5 PM
TERRAIN track
DATE Jan 5
WALK BREAK 400 m

COMMENTS
2:30
2:36
2:33 felt
2:37
Perform 2:32
2:36
My best workout in years!
- walked 400m between each
- struggled on last one
Achilles ached - iced 15 min
12 min warm up and warm down

Saturday
GOAL Off
TIME
DISTANCE
AM PULSE 55
WEATHER
TEMP
TIME AM PM
TERRAIN
DATE Jan 6
WALK BREAK

COMMENTS
Kids soccer (Morn)
* Westin scores goal bouncing off his back 1st goal of season!
Brennan's cross country (aft) Invitational
* Brennan comes from 8th to 3rd in the last half mile. I'm so proud!

Sunday
GOAL 18 mi (1) easy!
TIME 2:53
DISTANCE 18 mi
AM PULSE 52
WEATHER 50°
TEMP dry no wind
TIME AM PM
TERRAIN flat
DATE Jan 7
WALK BREAK 1 min / mi

COMMENTS
It was great to cover 18 miles — wish I had a group longest run in 18 months!
but...
* went too fast in the first 5 miles
* Achilles hurt afterward — take 3 days off
* Power Bar + water from 10 mi kept spirits up

* Pulse is up — I'm not recovering — need more days off/week

- Notebook

You don't need to have a commercial product. You can create your own journal by using a basic school notebook of your choice. Find one of the size that works best with your lifestyle (briefcase, purse, etc.); Below you will find the items that I've found helpful for most runners to record, but the best journals are those that make it easier for you to collect the data you find interesting, while allowing for creativity. The non-limiting nature of a notebook is a more comfortable format for runners who like to write a lot one day and not so much another day.

- Computer logs

There are a growing number of websites and software programs used by runners to record and track their training information. Some electronic devices (mostly GPS) allow you to download data and then sort it. As you set up your own codes and sections you can manage your training, identify trends, and plan ahead.

The planning process can reduce stress – and activate the conscious brain

1. Look over the full training schedule and make any changes needed to customize it for your use.
2. Write down the goal races, on the appropriate weeks in your journal. Use a hi-lighter or other method to make these weeks stand out.
3. Write down the assigned workouts for each day of each week for the next 4-8 weeks in pencil.
4. Look at each of the next 8 weeks quickly to make sure you don't have any trips, meetings, or family responsibilities that require adjusting the workouts.
5. Each week, add another week's workouts in pencil and note any changes in your travel, etc., schedule.
6. Each week, look ahead carefully at the next two weeks to ensure that the workouts are adjusted to your real-life schedule.

The data recording

1. As soon as you can, after a run, write the facts in your journal:
   - Mileage
   - Pace
   - Repetitions – times
   - Rest interval
   - Aches or pains – specifically where and how they hurt
   - Problems

In addition, you may also record:
- Time of run
- Total Time running
- Weather:
- Temp____
- Precipitation____
- Humidity____
- Run-Walk-Run frequency
- Any special segments of the run (speed, hills, race, etc.)
- Running companion
- Terrain
- How did you feel (1-10)
- Comments

2. Go back over the list again and fill in more details – emotional responses, changes in energy, location of aches and pains – even if they went away during the run. The more information you have, the more likely you are to find patterns that could indicate injury, blood sugar problems, lingering fatigue, as well as why you succeeded in certain races.

3. Helpful additions (usually in a blank section at the bottom of the page)
- Improvement thoughts
- Things I should have done differently
- Interesting happenings
- Funny things
- Strange things
- Stories, right brain crazy thoughts

Your morning pulse is a great guide of overstress

Recording morning pulse – immediately upon waking

1. As soon as you are conscious, but before you have thought much about anything count your pulse rate for a minute. Record it before you forget it. If you don't have your journal by your bed, then keep a piece of paper handy with a pen.

2. It is natural for there to be some fluctuations based upon the time you wake up, how long you have been awake, etc. But after several weeks and months, these will balance themselves out. The ideal would be to catch the pulse at the instant that you are awake, before the shock of an alarm clock, thoughts of work stress, etc.

3. After two weeks or so of readings, you can establish a baseline morning pulse. Remove the top high and low readings and then average the others.

4. The average is your guide. If, on a given day, the rate is 5% higher than your average, take an easy day. When the rate is 10% higher, and there is no reason for this (you woke up from an exciting dream, medication, infection, etc.) then your muscles may be tired indeed. Take the day off if you have a walk-run scheduled for that day.

5. If your pulse stays high for more than a week, call your doctor to see if there is a reason for this (medication, hormones, metabolic changes, infection, etc.). This could be due to overtraining.

17　Smooth Running Form Reduces Pain and Stress

I've known hundreds of runners who told me that they had to stop running because of pains in various parts of the body. After doing a running form evaluation, I found one or more problems with their running technique that were often the result of learning poor techniques when young. These bad habits can get hard-wired into the reflex brain. When an inefficient range of motion is repeated thousands of times every mile, some aches and pains often occur, thus producing stress.

But there's hope. When the form is corrected and the right drills are used to reinforce efficient movement, the aggravated area can heal, eliminating the pain. But there's something even more powerful going on. Monitoring running form and making adjustments activates the executive frontal lobe of the brain. The drills in the next chapter allow the conscious brain to retrain the reflex brain to activate efficient and smooth patterns.

Smooth running means using inertia

Your primary mission is to maintain momentum. Very little strength is needed to run – even in shorter races like the 800 meters. During the first hundred meters, you'll get your body into the motion and rhythm for your run. After that, the best strategy is to conserve energy while maintaining that forward momentum. To reduce fatigue, aches and pains, your right brain, helped by muscle memory, intuitively fine tunes your mechanics and motion to minimize effort.

Form mistakes add stress, produce aches and pains
1. Bouncing too much off the ground
2. Stride length too long
3. Leaning forward (unless this is natural for the individual)
4. Foot pushoff is not natural

Humans have many bio-mechanical adaptations working for them, which have been made more efficient over more than a million years of walking and running. The anatomical running efficiency of the human body originates in the ankle and achilles tendon, which I treat as a unit. This is no average body part, however, but an extremely sophisticated system of levers, springs, balancing devices, and more. Bio-mechanics experts believe that this degree of development was not needed for walking. When our ancient ancestors had to run to survive, the ankle/achilles adapted to endurance running/walking, producing a masterpiece of bio-engineering.

Through a series of speed sessions and drills, you can maximize use of the ankle so that a very little amount of muscle work produces a quicker, consistent forward movement. As you practice these, once a week, you'll be able to run farther and faster by using the techniques learned in these drills. Other muscle groups offer support and help to fine tune the process. When you feel aches and pains that might be due to the way you run, going back to the minimal and gentle use of the ankle and achilles tendon can often leave you feeling smooth and efficient very quickly.

- Wobbling: It all starts with general fatigue that stresses your weak links. For example, if your calf muscles become fatigued at the end of a workout or a race, and you keep pushing to maintain pace, your body will use other muscles and tendons to keep going. You start to "wobble" as these alternatives are not designed to do the job, stressing the knees, hips, IT band, back, glutes, hamstrings, etc. The longer you "wobble," the more prone you will be to injury.

- Stride extension when tired: There are several instincts that can hurt us. When tired, for example, many runners extend stride length to maintain pace. This may work for a while at the expense of the quads, hamstrings, and several other components that become over-stressed. It is always better, when you feel even a slight aggravation at the end of a run, to cut stride and get back into a smooth motion. It's OK to push through tiredness when running smoothly as long as you are not feeling pain in any area. But if this means extending stride or wobbling (which aggravates your weak links), you will pay for this.

    Be sensitive and avoid irritation: I don't suggest that everyone try to be a perfect runner. But when you become aware of your form problems, and make changes to become more efficient, you'll reprogram the reflex brain to a smoother motion, reducing aches and pains and lowering fatigue. This can also help you run faster.

When under stress, just use the ankle

Shorten stride, keep the feet low to the ground, touch lightly and the ankle will release in a reflex action, over and over and over. Very little energy is used with this motion. Practice this "fast shuffle" and you will program the reflex brain to run this way when needed.

Relaxed muscles, especially at the end of the run

Overall, the running motion should feel smooth, and there should be no tension in your neck, back, shoulders or legs. Even during the last half mile of a hard workout or race, try to maintain the three main elements of good form, and you'll stay relaxed: upright posture, feet low to the ground, and relaxed stride. You should not try to push through tightness and pain. Adjust your form to reduce aches and recovery time.

Tip: If you feel yourself tightening up, talk to the muscles, tendons, neck and back as you make form adjustments. Tell yourself to take a good breath and run like a "puppet on a string." This conscious act can help shift control to the conscious frontal brain and away from the reflex brain. As you do the "puppet" (or whatever helps you relax), you will be re-programming the reflex brain to do this automatically in the future. It may take dozens of retraining sessions to see this happening.

Three negative stresses of inefficient form

Most runners have an intuitive sense that something is wrong with their form but don't make corrections. The stress builds up and triggers negative attitude secretions.

1. Fatigue from extraneous motions becomes so severe that it takes much longer to recover.
2. Muscles or tendons are pushed beyond capabilities and break down, resulting in pain, injury or fatigue.
3. The experience is so negative that the desire to run is reduced, producing burnout.

The big three: Posture, Stride & Bounce

In thousands of individual running form consultations, I've discovered that when runners have problems, they tend to occur in these three running form components. Often the problems are like a signature, tending to be very specific to the areas that you overuse, because of your unique movement patterns. By making a few small changes in running form, most of the runners I've worked with have reduced or eliminated the source of the problems, even the source of pain (when present).

I. Posture

Good running posture is actually good body posture. The head is naturally balanced over the shoulders, which are aligned over the hips. As the foot comes underneath, all of these elements are in balance so that no energy is needed to prop up the body. You shouldn't have to work to pull a wayward body back from a wobble or an inefficient motion.

Forward lean – the most common mistake

Posture errors tend to be mostly due to a forward lean, especially when we are tired. The head wants to get to the finish as soon as possible, but the legs can't go any faster. A common tendency at the end of a speed session is to lean with the head. In races, this results in more than a few falls around the finish line. A forward lean will often concentrate fatigue, soreness and tightness in the lower back, or neck. Biomechanics experts note that a forward lean will reduce stride length, causing a slowdown and/or an increase in effort.

It all starts with the head. When the neck muscles are relaxed, the head can naturally seek an alignment that is balanced on the shoulders. If there is tension in the neck, or soreness afterward, the head may lean too far forward. This triggers a more general upper body imbalance in which the head and chest are suspended slightly ahead of the hips and feet. Sometimes, headaches result from this postural problem. Ask a running companion to tell you if and when your head is too far forward, or leaning down. This usually occurs at the end of a tiring run. The ideal position of the head is mostly upright, with your eyes focused about 30-40 yards ahead of you. Imagine that you are a "puppet on a string."

Sitting back

The hips are the other major postural component that can get out of alignment. A runner with this problem, when observed from the side, will have the butt behind the rest of the body. When the pelvic area is shifted back, the legs are not allowed to go through their ideal range of motion, and the stride length is shortened. This produces a slower pace, even when spending significant effort. Many runners tend to hit harder on their heels when their hips are shifted back, but this is not always the case.

A backward lean is rare

It is rare for runners to lean back, but it happens. In my experience, this is usually due to a structural problem in the spine or hips. If you lean backwards, and you're having pain in the neck, back or hips, you should see an orthopedist that specializes in the back. One symptom is excessive shoe wear on the back of the heel, but there are other reasons why you may show this kind of wear.

Correction: "Puppet on a string"

The best correction I've found to postural problems has been this mental image exercise: imagine that you are a puppet on a string. In other words, you're suspended from above, lifed from the head and each side of the shoulders. In this way, your head lines up above the shoulders, the hips come directly under, and the feet naturally touch lightly directly underneath. It won't hurt anyone to do the "puppet" several times during a run.

It helps to combine this image with a deep breath. After every 4-5 minutes, as you start to run after a walk break, exhale more than usual and inhale so that you divert air into the lower lungs. Every 3rd or 4th breath could be a lower lung breath. As you inhale, straighten up and say, "I'm a puppet." Then imagine that you don't have to spend energy maintaining this upright posture, because the "strings" attached from above keep you on track. As you continue to use this visualization, you'll reinforce good posture, and the behavior can be hardwired into your reflex brain.

Upright posture not only allows you to stay relaxed, but you will probably improve stride length. When you lean forward, you'll be reducing stride to stay balanced. When you straighten up, you'll receive a stride bonus of an inch or so, without any increase in energy. Note: don't try to increase stride length. When it happens naturally, you won't feel it.

An oxygen dividend

Breathing improves when you straighten up. A leaning body can't get ideal use out of the lower lungs. This can cause side pain. When you run upright, the lower lungs can receive adequate air, maximize oxygen absorption, and reduce the chance of side pain.

Note: Over the years, I've found a handful of runners who naturally run with a forward lean. If this is the way you've run and don't have any back, neck or other problems, continue. Each person should run the way that is natural and most run upright, according to my experience.

II.   Bounce

The most efficient stride is a shuffle with feet close to the ground. As long as you pick your foot up enough to avoid stumbling over a rock or uneven pavement, stay low. Most runners don't need to get more than 1" clearance, even when running fast. As you increase speed and ankle action, you will come off the ground a bit more than this. Again, don't try to increase stride, let this happen naturally.

Your ankle, combined with the achilles tendon, will act as a spring, moving you forward with each running step. If you stay low to the ground, very little effort is required. Through this "shuffling" technique, running becomes almost automatic. When runners err on bounce, they try to push off too hard. This usually results in extra effort spent in lifting the body off the ground. You can think of this as energy wasted in the air, energy that could be used to run faster at the end, when it counts.

The other negative force that "bouncers" experience is that of gravity. The higher you rise, the harder you fall. Each additional bounce off the ground delivers a lot more impact on feet and legs, which, during speed sessions, races, and long runs, produces aches, pains and injuries.

The correction for too much bounce: Light touch

The ideal foot "touch" should be so light that you don't usually feel yourself pushing off or landing. This means that your foot stays low to the ground and goes though an efficient and natural motion. Instead of trying to overcome gravity, you get in synch with it. If your foot "slaps" when you run, you will definitely improve with a lighter touch.

A "light touch drill":

During the middle of a run, time yourself for 20 seconds. Focus on one item: touching so softly that you don't hear your feet. Earplugs are not allowed for this drill. Imagine that you are running on thin ice or through a bed of hot coals. Do several of these 20 second touches, becoming quieter and quieter. You should feel very little impact on your feet as you do this drill.

III.   Stride

Studies have shown that as runners get faster, the stride length shortens. This clearly shows that the key to faster and more efficient running is increased cadence or quicker turnover of feet and legs. A major cause of aches, pains and injuries is a stride length that is too long. When in doubt, it is always better to err on the side of having a shorter stride.

Don't lift your legs!

Even most of the world class distance runners I've observed over the years don't have a high leg lift. When your legs rise too high, you will over-use the quadricep muscle (front of the thigh), resulting in a stride that is too long to be efficient. Many runners do this subconsciously at the end of long runs and races. The most common result is sore quadricep muscles for the next day or two.

Don't kick out too far in front of you!

If you watch the natural movement of the leg, it will kick forward slightly as the running foot gently moves forward, and then land underneath to make contact with the ground. Let this be a natural motion that leaves no tightness in the muscles behind the lower or upper leg.

Tightness in the front of the shin, behind the knee, or in the hamstring (back of the thigh) are signs that you are kicking too far forward and reaching out too far. Correct this by staying low to the ground, shortening the stride, and lightly touching the ground.

The following drills have helped thousands of runners run more efficiently and faster. Each develops different capabilities, and each rewards the individual for running smoother, reducing impact, using momentum, increasing the cadence or turnover of the feet and legs. With each drill, you'll be teaching yourself to move forward more directly and easily down the road.

When?

These should be done on a non-long run day. It is fine, however, to insert them into your warm-up, before a race or a speed workout. Many runners have also told me that both drills are a nice way to break up an average run that might otherwise be "boring."

Troubleshooting Form-Related Injuries

Lower back – Caused by forward lean, overstride, too few walk breaks

Neck pain – Caused by forward lean, head placed too far forward or back

Hamstring pain – Caused by striding too long, stretching

Shin pain on front – Caused by stride length too long, especially on downhills or at end of run

Shin pain on inside – Caused by over-pronation, uneven terrain

Achilles – Caused by stretching, speedwork, over-pronation

Calf pain – Caused by stretching, speedwork, inadequate number of walk breaks on long run

Knee pain – Caused by too few walk breaks, over-pronation, speedwork, extended stride

The "shuffle"

The most efficient and gentle running form is a "shuffle": the feet stay next to the ground, touching lightly with a relatively short stride. When running at the most relaxed range of the shuffling motion, the ankle mechanism does almost all of the work, and little effort is required from the calf muscle.

Speedwork increases injury risk

To improve, time goal runners need to run faster in some workouts, and this means some increase in stride length, greater bounce and foot pushing. By gradually increasing the intensity of speed training, the feet and legs can adapt (with sufficient rest intervals and rest days between). But there is still a risk of injury. Be sensitive to your weak links and don't keep running if there is the chance that you may have the beginnings of an injury. A gentle increase in the beginning of the season can significantly reduce risk.

Suggestions for running smoother, reducing irritation to weak links

- Feet low to the ground, using a light touch of the foot.
- Try not to bounce more than an inch off the ground.
- Let your feet move the way that is natural for them. If you tend to land on your heel and roll forward, do so.
- If you have motion control issues, an orthotic can provide minor correction to bring you into alignment and avoid irritating a weak. A supportive shoe is also needed.. Check with an experienced podiatrist about these issues.
- Legs – Maintain a gentle stride that allows your leg muscles to stay relaxed. In general, it's better to have a shorter stride and focus on quicker turnover if you want to speed up.
- Water running can help in reducing flips and turns of the feet and legs, which sometimes cause injuries, aches and pains. With a flotation device, run in the deep end of the pool so that your foot does not touch the bottom. Even one session of 15 minutes once a week can be beneficial.

18 THE DRILLS

CD – The Cadence Drill for Faster Turnover

This is an easy drill that helps you to become a smoother runner, using less effort. By doing it regularly, you pull all the elements of good running form together at the same time. One drill a week will help you step lightly as you increase the number of steps taken per minute. This will help you run faster with less effort.

1. Warm up by walking for 5 minutes, then running and walking very gently for 10 minutes.
2. Start jogging slowly for 1-2 minutes, and then time yourself for 30 seconds. During this half minute, count the number of times your left foot touches. Tip: Use a Run-Walk-Run Timer
3. Walk around for a minute or so.
4. On the 2nd 30-second drill, increase the count by 1 or 2.
5. Repeat this 3-7 more times, each time trying to increase by 1-2 additional steps.

In the process of improving turnover, the body's internal monitoring system coordinates a series of adaptations that make the feet, legs, nervous system and timing mechanism work together as an efficient team:

* Your foot touches more gently
* Extra, inefficient motions of the foot and leg are reduced or eliminated
* Less effort is spent on pushing up or moving forward
* You're lower to the ground – less impact
* The ankle becomes more efficient
* Ache and pain areas are not overused

Acceleration-Glider Drills

Many runners want to run faster but feel awkward and stressed when they try to do so. This is most often due to the lack of gentle training in faster running form. As one does the acceleration-glider regularly, runners find it easier to run faster and smoother. You'll use the conscious brain at the beginning of each of these drills, allowing for training of the reflex brain to repeat it smoothly 4-8 times.

This drill is a very easy and gentle form of speed play, or fartlek. By doing it regularly, you develop a range of speeds with the muscle conditioning to move smoothly from one to the next. The greatest benefit comes as you learn how to "glide" or coast off your momentum.

1. Done on a non-long-run day, in the middle of a shorter run, or as a warmup for a speed session, a race, or MM day.
2. Warm up with at least half a mile of easy running.
3. Many runners do the cadence drill just after the easy warmup, followed by the acceleration-gliders. But each can be done separately if desired.
4. Run 4-8 of them.
5. Do this at least once a week.
6. No sprinting, never run all-out.

After teaching this drill at my one-day running schools and weekend retreats for years, I can say that most people learn better through practice when they work on the concepts (rather than the details) of the drill. So just get out there and try them!

Gliding – The most important concept. This is like coasting off the momentum of a downhill run. You can do some of your gliders running down a hill if you want, but it is important to do at least two of them on flat terrain.

Do this every week – As in the cadence drills, regularity is very important. If you're like most runners, you won't glide very far at first. Regular practice will help you glide farther and farther.

Don't sweat the small stuff – I've included a general guideline of how many steps to do with each part of the drill, but don't worry about getting any set number of steps. It's best to get into a flow with this drill.

Smooth transition between each of the components. Each time you "shift gears," you are using the momentum of the current mode to start yourself into the next mode. Don't make a sudden and abrupt change, but have a smooth transition between modes.

Here's how it's done:
- Start by jogging very slowly for about 15 steps.
- Then jog faster for about 15 steps, increasing to a regular running pace for you.
- Now, over the next 25 steps or so, gradually increase the speed to your current race pace.
- OK, it's time to glide or coast. Allow yourself to gradually slow down to a jog using momentum as long as you can. At first, you may only glide for 10-20 steps. As the months go by, you will get up to 30 and beyond....you're gliding!

Overall purpose: As you do this drill every week, your form will become smoother at each mode of running. Congratulations! You are learning how to keep moving at a fairly fast pace without using much energy. This is the main object of the drill.

There will be some drills when you will glide longer than others – don't worry about this. By doing this drill regularly, you will find yourself coasting or gliding down the smallest of inclines, and even for 10-20 yards on the flat, on a regular basis. Gliding conserves energy, reduces soreness and fatigue, and helps you maintain a faster pace in races.

19 Hill Training for Strength and Race Preparation

Most of the runners I've coached who are stressed by hills in races have not done much (if any) hill training. As they worry about hills, the negative attitude hormones lower motivation. Running the workouts below, at least every 14 days, desensitizes one to the adversity of the hill. Most develop a hill technique that allows them to run on hilly courses without any more fatigue than flat courses. The regular insertion of hill workouts will instill a significant confidence that helps in every aspect of running and racing, reducing stress and boosting the effect of positive peptides.

Hill training strengthens the legs for running better than any other activity I know. At the same time, it can help you maximize an efficient stride length, increase leg speed, and improve your ability to run hills in races. The hill training workouts should not leave you exhausted. Over several weeks, hill work can gently introduce the feet, legs and cardiovascular system to faster running, while improving confidence.

The hill workout
- Length: beginners, 50-100 walking steps; advanced, 200-300 walking steps; those in-between these two levels, 100-200 walking steps.
- Walk for 2-3 minutes.
- Jog and walk to a hill – about 10 minutes. Beginners or runners making a "comeback" should jog a minute and walk a minute (a longer warm-up is fine) during the first few weeks of training.
- Do four acceleration-gliders. These are listed in the "Drills" chapter (don't sprint).
- Reverse this warm-up as your cool-down.
- Choose a hill with a moderate grade – steep hills often cause problems
- Run up the hill for 5 seconds, and then down for 5 seconds, gently. Walk for 10-15 seconds. Repeat this 5-10 times. This finalizes the warm-up.
- Walk for 2-3 minutes..
- Run the first few steps of each hill acceleration at a jog, then gradually pick up the turnover of the feet as you go up the hill.
- Get into a comfortable rhythm so that you can gradually increase this turnover (of steps per minute) as you go up the hill.
- Keep shortening stride length as you go up the hill.
- It's OK to huff and puff at the top of the hill (due to increased turnover and running uphill), but don't let the legs get over extended, or feel exhausted.

- Run over the top of the hill by at least 10 steps;
- Jog back to the top of the hill and walk down to recover between the hills. Walk as much as you need for complete recovery after each hill.

Hill training strengthens lower legs and improves running form

- Start with a comfortable stride, fairly short.
- As you go up the hill, shorten the stride.
- Touch lightly with your feet.
- Maintain a body posture that is perpendicular to the horizontal (upright, not leaning forward or back).
- Pick up the turnover of your feet as you go up and over the top.
- Keep adjusting stride so that the leg muscles don't tighten up. You want them as resilient as possible.
- Relax as you go over the top of the hill and glide (or coast) a bit on the downside.

Hill workout running form

The incline of the hill forces your legs to work harder as you go up. The extra work up the incline and the faster turnover builds strength. By taking an easy walk between the hills and an easy day afterward, the lower leg muscles rebuild stronger. Over several months, the improved strength allows you to support your body weight farther forward on your feet. An extended range of motion of the ankle and achilles tendon results in a "bonus" extension of the foot forward with no increase in effort. You will run faster without working harder. What a deal!

Running faster on hills in races

Maintain the the same breathing rate as you go up the hill, as when on the flat. As you go up the hill, you will shorten the stride. This reduces effort and allows most runners to maintain the same turnover rate of feet, as when on flat terrain. Once you train yourself to run with efficient hill form, you'll run faster with increased turnover on the hill workouts. This prepares you to do the same in races. You won't run quite as fast in a race as in your workouts, but through hill training, you train yourself to run faster than you used to run up the same hill on a race course.

Hill technique in a race is the same as in workouts: keep shortening stride as you move up the hill. Monitor your respiration rate: don't huff and puff more than you were doing on the flat. As runners improve their hill technique in races, they find that a shorter and quicker stride reduces effort while increasing speed. The technique is right for the individual when there is no increase in breathing rate even when the turnover rate is increased slightly.

Note: On your long runs and easy running days, just jog up hills, don't run faster up the hill. If your breathing is increasing on a hill, reduce effort and stride length until your respiration is as it was on the flat ground – or take more frequent walk breaks than when on the flat.

Downhill form

- Maintain a light touch of the foot
- Use an average stride or quick shuffle
- Keep feet low to the ground
- Let gravity pull you down the hill
- Turnover of the feet will pick up
- Try to glide (or coast) quickly down the hill

Biggest mistakes: too long a stride, bouncing too much

Even when the stride is one or two inches too long, your downhill speed can get out of control. If you are bouncing more than an inch or two off the ground, you'll risk pounding your feet, having to use your quads to slow down (producing soreness) and creating hamstring soreness due to overstride. The best indicators of overstride are tight hamstrings (big muscle behind your upper leg) and sore quads the next day. Using a quick and slightly shorter stride can allow one to run just as fast downhill as with a long stride, without sore quads, sore shins or aggravated hamstrings.

20 Mantras

Athletes have used key words or phrases for generations. These short statements shift control to the frontal lobe while they activate positive attitude hormones. Keep using them and you can push back the negative and increase the positive. Try these out during your runs so that you will feel comfortable with them. When needed, you'll be ready.

Have fun with these: Combine several that make you feel strong. Get into a rhythm. Make up a little lyric and sing them.

Mantras that work at any time

Don't give up

I can do it

This is my day

I feel good

I am strong

I have control

I'm getting it done

I feel confident

I'm running smooth

I will prevail

The spirit is strong

Talking to your workhorses

Heart – great pumping action

Heart – send the blood

Blood – bring the oxygen, bring the energy

Blood – remove the damage

Blood capillaries – open up, good flow

Feet – light touch

Feet – good turnover

Feet – quick and light

Feet – low to the ground

Muscles – pump the blood

Legs – staying strong

Legs – smooth motion

Knees – not perfect but working

Lungs – more oxygen

Lungs – working better

Lungs – cleaning the blood

Body – everything working together

Body – a smooth running machine

Endorphins – hit me

Endorphins – I feel good

Endorphins – flowing better

Endorphins – make me feel so good

Mind-body – great teamwork

Mind-body – getting it done

Mind-body – a powerful team

Mind-body – solving problems

Tight muscles – go awaylactic acid

Oxygen – go to the muscles

Sugar – go to the brain

Blood – flow, flow, flow

When it gets tough

One more mile

One more minute

One more step

I have reserve strength

I can do it

I feel empowered

I can push through fatigue

I am doing it

The finish is closer

The strength is there

The vision

I want to run

I am a runner

I am free

I can feel the accomplishment

Finish line – I feel it

The stress is leaving

The energy is increasing

The endorphins are flowing

I'm being pulled to the finish

I'm pulled along with the flow

The crowd is pushing

I'm getting energy from the crowd

There's energy moving together

I feel the energy of others

We're helping one another

I'm feeling stronger

I've got mental momentum

I've pushed through the wall

I'm going to finish with strength

I'm improving the quality of my life

I'm improving

I am better

I am fit

I'm running like Phidippides

I'm continuing the marathon tradition

2,500 years of history – I'm part of it

I'm smiling

I'm breathing life into my body

Distractions from negative thoughts

Where could I move that sign

How would I redesign that building

What type of house would I build here

Where would I live in this neighborhood

What role would that person play in my novel

What can I do to help that person get into running

Where would I put a running trail in this neighborhood

Talking to spectators and volunteers

Thank you for cheering

Thank you for being here

You can join us next year

Thanks for your energy

Thank you for helping me improve my life

Funny mantras

I'm running like (a funny character)

I'm dancing

I'm running on thin ice

Talking to the pain mantras (walk a bit more on the walk breaks and smile)

Brain, I know what you are doing

Open up blood flow to my (foot, leg, hamstring, etc.)

I feel better, now open up more blood

Blood flow, blood flow

Endorphins – flow in there

I need more endorphins – come on in

21 The Galloway Run-Walk-Run ™ Method

"The scheduled use of walk breaks gives each runner control over fatigue, reducing stress build-up."

- By determining a specific run-walk-run stategy, you activate the conscious brain
- This takes control away from the reflex brain
- Your control over this process reduces stress and activates positive attitude hormones
- You choose the length of a run segment – short enough so that you know you can do it
- This breaks up the longer event into segments that are do-able
- Walk breaks erase fatigue and reduce stress build-up
- Walk breaks reduce pain and lower stress
- During the walk break, you can enjoy the endorphin attitude boost

You are the one who determines how much you run and how much you walk

One of the wonderful aspects of running is that there is no definition of a "runner" that you must live up to. There are also no rules that you must follow as you do your daily run. You are the captain of your running ship, and it is you who determines how far, how fast, how much you will run, walk, etc. While you will hear many opinions on this, running has always been a freestyle type of activity in which each individual is empowered to mix and match the many variables and come out with the running experience that he or she chooses. Walk breaks can keep the first-time runner away from injury and burnout, and can help veterans to improve time. Here's how it works.

Walk before you get tired

Most of us, even when untrained, can walk for several miles before fatigue sets in because walking is an activity that we are bio-engineered to do for hours. Running is more work because you have to lift your body off the ground and then absorb the shock of the landing over and over. This is why continuous use of the running muscles will produce fatigue, aches, and pains much more quickly. If you insert a walk break into a run before your running muscles start to get tired, you allow the muscle to recover instantly, increasing your capacity for exercise while reducing the chance of next-day soreness.

The "method" part involves having a strategy, which allows the conscious brain to be in command. By using a ratio of running and walking, listed below, you will manage your fatigue. Using this fatigue-reduction tool early will save muscle resources and instill the mental confidence needed to cope with any challenges that may come later. Even when you don't need the extra muscle strength and resiliency bestowed by the method, you will feel better during and after your run, and finish knowing that you could have gone farther.

Beginners will primarily walk at first. By inserting short segments of running, followed by longer walk breaks, your muscles adapt to running without getting overwhelmed. As you improve your running ability, you will reach a point where you can set the ratio of running and walking for that day.

"The run-walk method is very simple: you run for a short segment and then take a walk break, and keep repeating this pattern."

Walk breaks allow you to take control over fatigue in advance so that you can enjoy every run. By taking them early and often, you can feel strong, even after a run that is very long for you. Beginners will alternate very short run segments with short walks. Even elite runners find that walk breaks on long runs allow them to recover faster. There is no need to reach the end of a run feeling exhausted if you insert enough walk breaks on that day.

Walk breaks

- Give you control over your fatigue and can virtually eliminate injury
- Give you confidence, stimulate positive attitude hormones
- Erase fatigue
- Push back your fatigue "wall"
- Allow for endorphins to collect during each walk break, improving attitude
- Break up the distance into manageable units ("one more minute until a walk break")
- Speed recovery
- Reduce the chance of aches, pains and injury (and the negative peptides they can bring)
- Allow you to feel good afterward, doing what you need to do without debilitating fatigue
- Give you all of the endurance of the distance of each session without the pain

A short and gentle walking stride

It's better to walk gently with a short stride. There has been some irritation of the shins when runners or walkers maintain a stride that is too long.

No need to eliminate the walk breaks

Some beginners assume that they must work toward the day when they don't have to take any walk breaks at all. This is up to the individual but is not recommended. Remember that you decide what ratio of run-walk-run to use. There is no rule that requires you to run any ratio of run-walk on any given day. I suggest that you adjust the ratio according to how you feel.

I've run for over 50 years and enjoy running more than ever because of walk breaks. Each run I take energizes my day. I would not be able to run almost every day if I didn't insert walk breaks early and often. I start most runs taking a short walk break every minute.

How to keep track of the walk breaks

There is now a Galloway timer that beeps and/or vibrates (about $20). There are also several watches that can be set to beep when it's time to walk and then beep again when it's time to start up again. Check our website (www.jeffgalloway.com) or a good running store for advice in this area.

How to use walk breaks

1. Beginners usually start by running for 5-10 seconds, then walking for the rest of each minute.
2. Veterans can use the guide below, based upon pace per mile, to set up the walk breaks. If you feel good during and after the run, continue with this ratio. If not, run less until you feel good.
3. When challenged, decrease the run amount and increase the walk
4. On long runs, take walk breaks a lot more freqently to speed up recovery.
5. Veterans can reduce or eliminate walk breaks during the last 25% of their races.

Walk breaks strategies

The frequency of walk breaks is usually tied to the pace per mile. But it is always OK to walk more frequently if you want to do so. Here are the current strategies:

- 8 min/mi – run 4 minutes/walk 30 seconds
- 9 min/mi – run 4 min/walk 1 min (4/1)
- 10 min/mi – 3/1
- 11 min/mi – 2:30/1
- 12 min/mi – 2/1
- 13 min/mi – 1/1
- 14 min/mi – 30 sec/30 sec
- 15 min/mi – 30 sec run/45 sec walk
- 16 min/mi – 20 sec run/40 sec walk
- 17 min/mi – 15 sec run/45 sec walk
- 18 min/mi – 10 sec run/50 sec walk

22 Good Blood Sugar = Motivation

Your blood sugar level (BSL) determines how good you feel or can be a source of stress. Blood sugar fuels the brain, and the brain monitors this carefully. When the level gets even a bit too low, negative peptides increase, lowering motivation. When BSL is adequate, the receptor cells receive good messages and positive attitude hormones transmit positive messages throughout the mind-body. If you eat too much sugar, starch or other simple carbohydrates, your BSL can rise too high. You'll feel really good for a while, but the excess sugar triggers a release of insulin, which can push BSL too low. In this state, your reflex brain is under stress and reduces blood flow to the frontal lobe, resulting in foggy thinking. If the BSL is not raised, negative peptides are produced, lowering motivation and energy level.

When BSL is maintained at a stable level throughout the day, you will be more motivated to do most activities, including exercise. You'll have a more positive mental attitude and will be more likely to deal with stress and solve problems. Just as eating at regular intervals throughout the day maintains metabolism, the steady infusion of balanced nutrients all day long will maintain stable blood sugar, sending positive peptide messages throughout the body-mind that everything is OK.

Note: See *A Woman's Guide to Running/Fatburning* for more meal planning information.

If your BSL is low, the simple act of eating a snack containing 80% simple carbohydrates and about 20% protein, 30 minutes or less before your workout, will stimulate positive peptides, improving attitude and helping you to get out the door.

Eating every 2-3 hours is best

When exercisers experiment with various snacks, most find that an individualized arrangement of small meals produces a more stable BSL.

Do I have to eat before a workout? Only if the BSL is low

Most who exercise in the morning don't need to eat anything before the start. As mentioned above, if your blood sugar level is low in the afternoon, and you have a workout scheduled, a BSL snack can help. If you feel that a morning snack will help, the only issue is to avoid consuming so much that you get an upset stomach.

For best results in raising blood sugar when it is too low (within 30 minutes before exercise), try different snacks. The product Accelerade has worked best among the thousands of exercisers I hear from every year. It has the 80%/20% ratio of carb to protein. If you eat an energy bar with the 80/20 ratio, be sure to drink 6-8 oz of water at the same time.

Eating during exercise

Most exercisers don't need to worry about eating or drinking during a run or walk until the length of the session exceeds 60 minutes (for most of my clients, 90 minutes). At this point, there are several options.

- On runs longer than an hour, many runners like to use a BSL booster. Practice various eating strategies on your long walks/runs and pick what works best.
- Rule of thumb: 30-40 calories every 2 miles.
- Gel products – these come in small packets, and are the consistency of honey or thick syrup. The most successful way to take them is to put 1-2 packets into a small plastic bottle with a pop-top. About every 10-15 minutes, take a squirt or two with a sip or two of water.
- Energy bars – Cut a bar into 8-10 pieces and take a piece, with a couple of sips of water, every 10-15 minutes.
- Candy/sugar – Gummi bears, Life Savers, sugar cubes, etc., when consumed during exercise, have produced the quickest boosting effect, among the runners I've monitored. The usual consumption is 30-40 calories, about every 10-15 minutes
- Sports drinks – Since there is a significant percentage of nausea episodes among those who drink these during exercise, this is not my top recommendation. If you have found that a product works for you, use it exactly as you have used it before.

It is important to reload after exercise within 30 minutes

Whenever you have finished a hard or long workout, a reloading snack of 100-300 calories will help you recover faster. Products with 80% simple carbs and 20% protein have been shown to be most successful in reloading the muscles. The product that has worked best among the thousands I work with each year is Endurox R4.

23 Troubleshooting

Knowing That There is a Solution to a Problem Reduces Stress and Improves Attitude

- Coming back after a layoff from running
- It hurts!
- No energy
- Side pain
- I feel great one day, but the next day...
- No motivation
- Cramps in my leg muscles
- Upset stomach or diarrhea
- Headache
- Should I run when I have a cold?
- Street safety
- Dogs
- Heart disease and running

How do I start back when I've had time off?

Many runners who take time off from running feel stressed when they start back. When the stress is high, the reflex brain triggers a series of actions that reduce motivation, including reduction of blood flow to key muscles, the brain, and the gut. It will also trigger negative attitude hormones that reduce motivation further. The longer you've been away from running, the greater the benefit from a plan that will allow the conscious brain to assume control over the anxiety-ridden reflex brain.

The use of walk breaks greatly improves confidence and attitude. Success is increased when one believes in the plan and takes conscious involvement to get out the door, as in the "Situations" chapter earlier in this book. I want to warn you now that you will reach a point when you feel totally back in shape, but you are not. Stay with the plan below for your return and, when in doubt, be more conservative. Remember that you are in this for the long run!

Note: I suggest using the proven training schedules in my books *Marathon, Year Round Plan, Galloway Training Programs, 5K/10K, Half Marathon, Cross Country Getting Started or Testing Yourself.* Each week's workouts are numbered in sequence, leading to the goal.

Less than 2 weeks off – You will feel like you are starting over again but should come back quickly. Look at the schedules. Let's say that you were at week 20 but had to take 10 days off. Start back at week 2 for the first week. If all is well, skip to week 10 or 11 for the second week. If that works well, ease into week 17 or 18 and then move back into week 20.

14 days to 29 days off – You will also feel like you are starting over again, and it will take longer to get it all back. Within about 5-6 weeks, you should be back to normal. Use the schedule of your choice (from week 1) for two weeks. If there are no aches, pains or lingering fatigue, then use the schedule but skip every other week. After the 5th week, transition back into what you were doing before the layoff.

One month or more off – If you have not run for a month or more, start over again like a beginner. Use one of the schedules, following it exactly (from week 1) for the first few weeks. After 2-3 weeks, the safest plan is to continue with the schedule. But if you're having no aches or pains, nor lingering fatigue, you could increase more rapidly by skipping one week out of three. After 2 months of no problems, your conditioning should have returned.

It hurts! Is it just a passing ache, or a real injury?

Most of the aches and pains, felt when running, are temporary body adjustments, don't indicate a serious problem and will go away within a few minutes. Research shows that runners over the age of 50 have fewer orthopedic problems compared with non-runners the same age. But if you try to run when there is a potential injury, you can make the ache worse, requiring more time for recovery.

If the pain comes on when running, just walk for an additional 2 minutes, jog a few strides, and walk another 2 minutes. If it still hurts after doing this 4 or 5 times, stop running and walk. If the pain goes away when you walk, just walk for the rest of the workout.

Walking pain – When the pain stays around when walking, use a very short stride. Walk slowly for 30-60 seconds. If it still hurts when walking, sit down and massage the area that hurts, if you can. Sit for 2-4 minutes. When you try again to walk, and it still hurts, call it a day – your workout is over.

It's an injury if...

There's inflammation – swelling in the area

There's loss of function – the foot, knee, etc., doesn't work correctly

There's pain – it hurts and keeps hurting or gets worse

Treatment suggestions

1. See a doctor who has treated other runners very successfully and wants to get you back on the road or trail.
2. Take at least 2-5 days off from any activity that could irritate it to get the healing started, more if needed.
3. If the area is next to the skin (tendon, foot, etc.), rub a chunk of ice on the area(s) constantly rubbing for 15 min until the area gets numb. Continue to do this for a week after you feel no symptoms. Ice bags and gel ice do virtually no good at all according to my experience.
4. If the problem is inside a joint or muscle, call your doctor and ask if you can use prescription strength anti-inflammatory medication. Don't take any medication without a doctor's advice and follow the advice you receive.
5. If you have a muscle injury, see a veteran sports massage therapist. Try to find one who has a lot of successful experience treating the area where you are injured. The magic fingers and hands can often work wonders.
6. Read the section on TMS in this book. A high percentage of runner's aches and pains come from TMS, which can be dealt with. See the TMS section in this book, page 65.
7. Belief in treatment mode can energize your organism for healing and increase positive peptides.

This is advice from one runner to another. For more info on injuries, treatment, etc., see a doctor and read *Running Injuries – Care and Prevention* by Hannaford and Galloway.

No energy today

There will be a number of days each year when you will not feel like exercising. On most of these, you can turn it around and feel great. Occasionally, you will not be able to do this because of an infection, lingering fatigue, or other physical problems. Here's a list of things that can give you energy. If these actions don't lead you to a run, then read the nutrition sections (particularly the blood sugar chapter) in this book or in *A Woman's guide to Fat-Burning* or *Galloway's Book on Running, Second Edition*.

1. Eat an energy bar, with water or caffeinated beverage, about an hour before the run. Caffeine helps!

2. Thirty minutes before exercising, you could drink 100-200 calories of a sports drink that has a mix of 80% simple carbohydrates and 20% protein. The product Accelerade already has this ratio.

3. Just walk for 5 minutes away from your house, office, etc., and the energy often kicks in. Forward movement gets the attitude moving, too.

4. One of the prime reasons for no energy is not reloading within 30 minutes after your last exercise session: 200-300 calories of a mix that is 80% simple carbohydrate and 20% protein (Endurox R4 is a product that has this formulation).

5. Low carb diets will result in low energy, low blood sugar level and low motivation before and during a workout.

6. In most cases, it is fine to keep going even if you aren't energetic. But if you sense an infection, see a doctor. If the low energy stays around for several weeks, see a nutritionist who knows about the special needs of runners and/or get some blood work done. This may be due to inadequate iron, B vitamins, protein, energy stores, etc.

Note: If you have any problems with caffeine, don't consume any products containing it. As always, if you sense any health problem, see a doctor.

Side pain

This is very common and usually has a simple fix. Normally, one should not worry about this, it just hurts. This condition is due to: 1) the lack of lower lung breathing; and 2) going a little too fast at the beginning of the run. You can correct #2 easily by walking more at the beginning and slowing down your running pace for the first 10 minutes of the run.

Lower lung breathing from the beginning of a run can prevent side pain. This way of inhaling air is performed by diverting the air you breathe into your lower lungs. Also called "belly breathing" this is how we breathe when asleep and provides maximum opportunity for oxygen absorption. If you don't breathe this way from the start of the run, and you are not getting the oxygen you need, the side pain will tell you. By slowing down, walking, and breathing deeply for a while, the pain may go away. But sometimes it does not. Most runners just continue to run and walk with the side pain. In 50 years of running and helping others run, I've not seen any lasting negative effect from those who run with side pain. You can prevent this by breathing properly.

A maximum breath is not needed. Simply breathe a normal breath but send it to the lower lungs. You know that you have done this if your stomach goes up and down as you inhale and exhale. If your upper chest goes up and down, you are not bringing a lot of air into the lower lungs.

Note: Never breathe in and out rapidly. This can lead to hyperventilation, dizziness, and fainting.

I feel great one day ... and not the next day

If you can solve this problem, you could become a very wealthy person. There are a few common reasons for this, but there will always be "those days" when the body doesn't seem to work right (gravity seems heavier than normal) and you cannot find a reason.

1. Pushing through. In most cases, this is a one-day occurrence. Most runners just put more walking into the mix and get through it. Before pushing, however, make sure that you don't have a medical reason for why you feel bad. Don't exercise when you have a lung infection, for example.

2. Heat and/or humidity will make you feel worse. You will often feel great when the temperature is below 60F and miserable when 80F or above (especially at the end of the workout). During hot periods, try to exercise before the sun gets above the horizon.

3. Low blood sugar can make any run a bad run. You may feel good at the start and suddenly feel like you have no energy. Every step seems to take a major effort. Read the chapter in this book about this topic.

4. Low motivation. Use the rehearsal techniques in the "Situations" section to get you out the door on a bad day. These have helped numerous runners turn their minds around, even in the middle of a run.

5. Infection can leave you feeling lethargic, achy, and unable to run at the same pace that was easy a few days earlier. Check the normal signs (fever, chills, swollen lymph glands, etc.) and at least call your doctor if you suspect something.

6. Medication and alcohol, even when taken the day before, can leave a hangover that dampens a workout.

7. A slower start can make the difference between a good day and a bad day. When your body is on the edge of fatigue or other stress, it only takes a few seconds too fast per mile, walking and/or running to push into discomfort or worse.

Cramps in the muscles

At some point, most runners experience cramps. These muscle contractions usually occur in the feet or the calf muscles and may come during a run or walk, or they may hit at random. Most commonly, they will occur at night, when you are sitting around at your desk or watching TV in the afternoon or evening.

If you are dehydrated at the start of your run, you are more likely to experience cramps. Avoid alcohol and salty food, and hydrate well the day before a long run. A good sports drink like Accelerade, taken throughout the day before, will help to keep your fluid levels and your electrolytes "topped off"(maximum of 16 oz per day).

When one has had several cramping episodes or one severe experience, the reflex brain remembers. For several weeks afterward, the reflex brain will trigger negative attitude peptides when you think about running. It is also possible that the reflex brain has reduced blood flow to the muscles in response to the stress. See the "Situations" chapter for ways of getting back into the flow of running.

Cramps vary in severity. Most are mild, but some can grab so hard that they shut down the muscles and hurt when they seize up. Massage and a short and gentle movement of the muscle can help to bring most of the cramps around. Odds are that stretching will make the cramp worse or tear the muscle fibers. There may be soreness in the cramped muscles for several days. On the short running days, take a longer walk as a warm-up and adjust the run-walk-run ratio to include more walking.

Most cramps are due to overuse, exercising farther or faster than in the recent past, or continuing to put yourself at your limit, especially in warm weather. Look at the pace and distance of your runs and run-walk-run strategy in your training journal to see if you have been running too far, too fast, or have not taken walk breaks liberally enough.

- Continuous running increases cramping. Taking walk breaks more often can reduce or eliminate cramps. Many runners who used to cramp when they ran a minute and walked a minute, stopped cramping with a ratio of run 30 seconds and walk 30-60 seconds.
- When a cramp has occurred, it may be necessary to do a "shuffle" break instead of taking a walk break. Shuffling is a minimal running motion in which the ankle is providing most of the energy and propulsion: short stride, feet next to the ground, light touch.

- Prolonged dehydration. Drink eight 7-ounce glasses of water a day plus one or two glasses of either electrolyte beverage or orange juice. During hot weather, a good electrolyte beverage can help to replace the salts that your body loses in sweating. A drink like Accelerade, for example, can help to top off these minerals after a very long run. Drink approximately 6-8 oz every 1-2 hours.

- On very long hikes, walks or runs, however, the continuous sweating, especially when drinking a lot of fluid, can push your sodium levels too low and produce muscle cramping. If this happens regularly, a buffered salt tablet can help greatly: Succeed is used by many runners in ultramarathons and Ironman events.

- Many medications, especially those designed to lower cholesterol, have muscle cramps as one of their known side effects. Runners who use medications and experience muscle cramps should ask their doctor if there are alternatives.

Here are several ways of dealing with cramps:
1. Take a longer and more gentle warm-up
2. When you start running, go slower
3. Shorten your run segment
4. Slow down your walk and walk more
5. Shorten your distance on a hot/humid day
6. Break your run up into two segments
7. Look at any other exercise that could be causing the cramps
8. Take a buffered salt tablet at the beginning of your exercise
9. Shorten your stride, especially on hills

Note: If you have high blood pressure, ask your doctor before taking any salt product.

Upset stomach or diarrhea

Nausea & diarrhea (N/D) are triggered by stress. Most commonly, it is the stress of running on that day due to the causes listed below. But stress can come from many unique conditions within the individual. Your reflex brain triggers the N/D to get you to reduce the exercise, which will reduce at least one source of stress. Here are the common causes.

1. **Running too fast or too far** is the most common cause. Runners are confused about this because the pace doesn't feel too fast in the beginning. Each person has a level of fatigue that triggers these conditions. Slowing down and taking more walk breaks from the beginning will help you manage the problem.

2. **Eating too much or too soon before the run.** Your system has to work hard when you're running and works hard to digest food. Doing both at the same time raises stress and results in nausea, etc. Having food in your stomach in the process of being digested is an extra stress and a likely target for elimination.

3. **Eating a high-fat or high-protein diet.** Even one meal that has over 50% of the calories in fat or protein can lead to N/D 1-4 hours later if you are running.

4. **Eating too much the afternoon or evening on the day before.** A big evening meal will still be in the gut being digested the next morning. When you bounce up and down on a run, which you will, you add stress to the system, often producing (N/D).

5. **Heat and humidity** are major causes of these problems. Some people don't adapt to heat well and experience N/D with minimal build-up of temperature or humidity. But in hot conditions, everyone has a core body temperature increase that will result in significant stress to the system often causing nausea and sometimes diarrhea. By slowing down, taking more walk breaks, and pouring water over your head, you can manage this better. The best time to exercise in warm weather is before the sun gets above the horizon.

6. **Drinking too much water *before* a run.** If you have too much water in your stomach and you are bouncing around, you increase stress on the digestive system. Reduce your intake to the bare minimum (one 4-6 oz portion, right after getting out of bed). Most runners don't need to drink any fluid before a run that is 60 minutes or less.

7. **Drinking too much of a sugar/electrolyte drink.** Water is the easiest substance for the body to process. The addition of sugar and/or electrolyte minerals, as in a sports drink, makes the substance harder to digest for many runners. During a run (especially on a hot day), it is best to drink only water. Cold water is best.

8. **Drinking too much fluid too soon *after* a run.** Even if you are very thirsty, don't gulp down large quantities of any fluid. Try to drink no more than 6-7 oz, every 20 minutes or so. If you are particularly prone to N/D, just take 2-4 sips every 5 minutes

or so. When the body is very stressed and tired, it's not a good idea to consume a sugar drink. The extra stress of digesting the sugar can lead to problems.

Don't let running be stressful to you. Some runners get too obsessed about inserting a run into every single day or running at a specific pace. This adds stress to your life. Relax and let your run diffuse some of the other tensions in your life.

Headache

There are several reasons why runners get headaches on runs. While uncommon, they happen to the average runner about 1-5 times a year. The extra stress that running puts on the body can trigger a TMS headache on a tough day, even considering the relaxation that comes from the run. Many runners find that a dose of an over-the-counter headache medication takes care of the problem. As always, consult with your doctor about use of medication. Here are some major causes/solutions.

Dehydration – If you run in the morning, make sure that you hydrate well the day before. Avoid alcohol if you run in the mornings and have headaches. Also, watch the salt in your dinner meal the night before. A good sports drink, like Accelerade, taken throughout the day before, will help to keep your fluid levels and electrolytes "topped off" (maximum of 16 oz per day). If you run in the afternoon, follow the same advice leading up to your run on the day of the run.

Medications can often produce dehydration – There are some medications that make runners more prone to headaches. Check with your doctor.

Too hot for you – Run at a cooler time of the day (usually in the morning before the sun gets above the horizon). When on a hot run, pour water over your head. Take more frequent walk breaks.

Running a little too fast – Start all runs more slowly, walk more during the first half of the run

Running farther than you have run in the recent past – Monitor your mileage and don't increase more than about 15% farther than you have run on any single run in the past week.

Low blood sugar level – Be sure to boost your BLS with a snack, about 30-60 min before you run. If you are used to having it, caffeine in a beverage can sometimes help this situation also.

If prone to migraines – There are many individual issues here. Try your best to avoid dehydration. Talk to your doctor about other possibilities. Read the section on TMS.

Watch your neck and lower back – If you have a slight forward lean as you run, you can put pressure on the spine, particularly in the neck and lower back. Read the form chapter in this book and run upright. Be a "puppet on a string."

Should I run when I have a cold?

Talk to your doctor when you have an infection –There are many individual health issues. Usually you will be given the OK to gently exercise.

Lung infection – Don't run! A virus in the lungs can move into the heart and kill you. Lung infections are usually indicated by coughing.

Common Cold? There are many infections that initially seem to be a normal cold but are not. At least call your doctor's office to get clearance before running. Be sure to explain how much you are running and what, if any, medication you are taking.

Throat infection and above – Most runners will be given the OK, but check with the doctor.

Street safety

Each year ,several runners are hit by cars when running. Most of these are preventable. Here are the primary reasons and what you can do about them.

1. The driver is intoxicated or preoccupied by cell phone, etc.

    Always be on guard – Even when running on the sidewalk or pedestrian trail. Many fatal crashes occurred when the driver lost control of the car and came up behind the runner on the wrong side of the road. I know it is wonderful to be on "cruise control" in your right brain, but you can avoid a life- threatening situation if you keep looking around and anticipate trouble. Wear a blinking light or reflective gear after dark. I recommend the NiteBeams products.

2. The runner dashes across an intersection against the traffic light.

    When running or walking with another person, don't try to follow blindly across an intersection. Runners who quickly sprint across the street without looking are often surprised by cars coming from unexpected directions. The best rule is the one that you heard as a child: When you get to an intersection, stop and see what the traffic situation is. Look both ways and look both ways again (and again) before crossing. Have an option to bail out of the crossing if a car surprises you from any direction.

3. Sometimes, runners wander out into the street as they talk and run.

    One of the very positive aspects of running becomes a negative one in this case. Yes, chat and enjoy time with your friends. But every runner in a group needs to be responsible for his or her own safety, footing, etc. Runners at the back of a group assume (mistakenly) that they don't have to be concerned about traffic at all. This results in a very risky situation.

    - In general, be ready to save yourself from a variety of traffic problems by following the rules below and any others that apply to specific situations. Even though the rules below seem obvious, many runners who are hit by cars tend to ignore them.

    - Be constantly aware of vehicular traffic at all times.

    - Assume that all drivers are drunk or crazy, or both. When you see a strange movement by a car, be ready to get out of the way.

    - Mentally practice running for safety. Get into the practice of thinking ahead at all times, with a plan for that current stretch of road.

    - Run as far off the road as you can. If possible, run on a sidewalk or pedestrian trail.

    - Run facing traffic. A high percentage of traffic deaths come from those who run with the flow of traffic and do not see the threat from behind.

    - Wear lights or reflective gear at night. NiteBeams have several products that blink and provide great protection.

    - Take control over your safety – You are the only person who can best protect yourself.

Dogs

When you enter a dog's territory, you may be in for a confrontation. Here are my suggestions for dealing with your "dog days".

1. There are several good devices that will help deter dogs: a stick, rocks, some electronic signal devices, and pepper spray. If you are in a new area, or an area of known dogs, I recommend that you have one of these at all times.

2. At the first sign of a dog ahead (or barking), try to figure out where the dog is located, whether the dog is a real threat, and what territory the dog is guarding.

3. The best option is to run a different route.

4. If you really want or need to run past the dog, pick up a rock if you don't have another anti-dog device.

5. Watch the tail. If the tail does not wag, beware.

6. As you approach the dog, it is natural for the dog to bark and head toward you. Raise your rock as if you will throw it at the dog. In my experience, the dog withdraws about 90% of the time. You may need to do this several times before getting through the dog's territory. Keep your arms up.

7. In a few cases, you will need to throw the rock (and sometimes another), if the dog keeps coming.

8. In less that 1% of the hundreds of dog confrontations I've had, there is something wrong with the dog, and it continues to move toward you. Usually the hair will be up on the dog's back. Try to find a barrier to get behind, yell loudly in hopes that the owner or someone will help you. If a car comes by, try to flag down the driver, and either stay behind the car as you get out of the dog's territory or get in the car for protection if that is appropriate.

9. Develop your own voice. Some use a deep commanding voice, some use a high-pitched voice. Whichever you use, exude confidence and command.

24 Injury Troubleshooting

NOTE: For more information see *Prevention and Care of Running Injuries,* by Hannaford and Galloway, available at www.JeffGalloway.com

Quick Treatment Tips

For all injuries
- Read the section on TMS in this book, page 65
- Take 3 days off from running or any activity that could aggravate the area
- Avoid any activity that could aggravate the injury
- As you return to running, stay below the threshold of further irritation with much more liberal walking
- Don't stretch. Stretching keeps most injuries from healing. Iliotibial stretches, however, can sometimes allow for running when the I-T band tightens up.

Muscle injuries
1. Call your doctor's office and see if you can take prescription strength anti-inflammatory medication
2. See a sports massage therapist who has worked successfully on many runners

Tendon and foot injuries
1. Rub a chunk of ice directly on the area for 15 minutes every night (keep rubbing until the area gets numb, about 15 minutes)

   Note: Ice bags or gel ice don't seem to help according to my experience

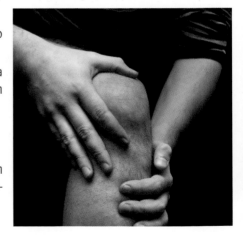

2. Foot injuries sometimes are helped by a "boot" cast at first to let the problem start healing

Knee injuries
1. Call your doctor's office to see if you can take prescription-strength anti-inflammatory medication

2. See if you can do a little gentle walking, sometimes this helps

3. Sometimes knee straps can relieve pain, ask your doctor

4. Get a shoe check to see if you are in the right shoe (if you over-pronate, a motion control shoe may help)

5. If you ove-pronate, an orthotic may help

6. If you have internal knee pain, a glucosamine supplement may help

7. If you have an iliotibial band injury, using a foam roller has helped. Roll for 5 minutes before bed and, if possible, 5 minutes both before and after a run.

Shin injuries

1. Rule out a stress fracture. In this case, the pain usually gets worse as you run, but chock with your doctor. If it is a stress fracture, you must stop running for (usually) at least 8 weeks.

2. If the pain gradually goes away as you run on it, there is less worry of a stress fracture. This is probably a shin splint. If you stay below the threshold of irritating the shin muscle, you can run with shin splints as they gradually go away (check with doctor to be sure).

3. Take more walk breaks, run more slowly, etc.

Starting running before the injury has healed

With most running injuries, you can continue to run even while the injury is healing. But first, you must have some time off to get the healing started. If you do this at the beginning of an injury you will usually only need 2-5 days off. The longer you try to push through the problem, the more damage you produce and the longer it will take to heal. Stay in touch with the doctor at any stage of this healing/running process, follow his/her advice, and use your best judgement.

To allow for healing, once you have returned to running, stay below the threshold of further irritation. In other words, if the injury feels a little irritated when running at 2.5 miles and starts hurting a little at 3 miles, you should run no more than 2 miles. And if your run-walk ratio is 3 min run/1 min walk, you should drop back to 1-1, or 30 seconds/30 seconds.

Take a day of rest between running days. With most injuries, but you can cross train to maintain conditioning, but make sure that your injury will allow this. Again, your doctor can advise.

Best cross training modes to maintain your running conditioning

Before doing any of these, ask your doctor. Most are fine for most injuries, but some run a risk of irritating the injured area and delaying the healing process. For more information on this, see the chapter on cross training, in my *Galloway's Book on Running, Second Edition*. Gradually build up the cross training because you have to condition those muscles gradually also. Even walking is a great way to maintain conditioning if the injury and the doctor will allow it.

1. Running in the water can improve your running form
2. Nordic Track machines
3. Walking
4. Rowing machines
5. Eliptical machines

See a doctor for medical issues.

25 Treatment Suggestions – from One Runner to Another

Taking some action to get the healing started and then treating it will build confidence, produce positive attitude peptides and mobilize your body, mind and spirit for healing. Believing in the treatment will also help.

Note: For more information, see *Prevention And Care Of Running Injuries*, by Hannaford and Galloway, available at www.JeffGalloway.com

Knee Pain

Most knee problems will go away if you take 5 days off. Ask your doctor if you can use anti-inflammatory medication. Try to figure out what caused the knee problem. Make sure that your running courses don't have a slant or canter. Look at the most worn pair of shoes you have, even walking shoes. If there is wear on the inside of the forefoot, you probably overpronate. If you have repeat issues with knee pain, you may need a foot support or orthotic. If there is pain under the kneecap, or arthritis, the glucosamine/chondroitin products have helped. The best I've found in this category is Joint Maintenance Product by Cooper Complete.

Outside of the knee pain – Iliotibial Band Syndrome

This band of fascia acts as a tendon, going down the outside of the leg from the hip to just below the knee. The pain is most commonly felt on the outside of the knee, but can be felt anywhere along the I-T band. I believe this to be a "wobble injury." When the running muscles get tired, they don't keep you on a straight running track. The I-T band tries to restrain the wobbling motion, but it cannot and gets overused. Most of the feedback I receive from runners and doctors is that once the healing has started (usually a few days off from running), most runners will heal as fast when you run on it as from a complete layoff. It is crucial to stay below the threshold of further irritation. Stay in touch with your doctor.

Treatment for iliotibial band:

1. Self-massage using a foam roller. This device has helped thousands of runners get over I-T band. On my website www.RunInjuryFree.com is a picture of someone using a foam roller. Put the roller on the floor, lie on it using body weight to press and roll the area that is sore. It helps to warm up the area before a run and to roll it out afterward. Especially helpful is to roll it 5 minutes before bed.

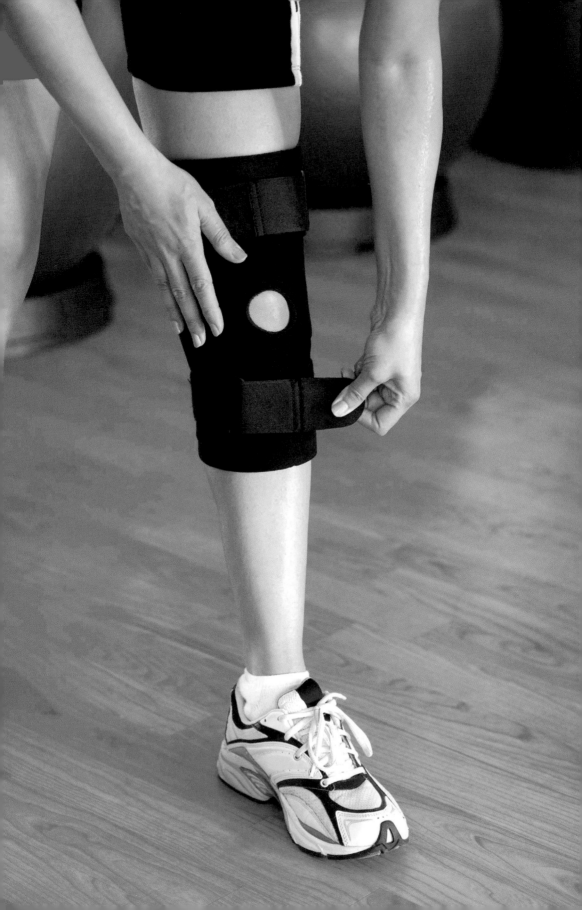

2. Massage Therapy: A good massage therapist can usually tell whether massage will help and where to massage. The two areas for possible attention are the connecting points of the connective tissue that is tight and the fascia band itself, in several places. "The stick" is a self-massage roller device that has also helped many runners recover from I-T band syndrome as they run. As with the foam roller, it helps to warm up the area before a run and to roll it out afterward.

3. Walking is usually fine, and usually you can find a run-walk ratio that works.

4. Direct ice massage on the area of pain: 15 minutes of continuous rubbing every night

5. Stretching: Stretch during a run if the I-T band tightens up. There are several stretches that have worked for this injury.

Shin pain – "Shin splints" or stress fracture

Almost always, pain in this area indicates a minor irritation called "shin splints" that allows running and walking as you heal. The greatest pain or irritation during injury is usually felt during the start of a run or walk, which gradually lessens or goes away as you run and walk. It takes a while to fully heal, so you must have patience as you stay below the threshold of further irritation.

• Inside pain – Posterior shin splints. Irritation of the inside of the leg, coming up from the ankle is called "posterior tibial shin splints" and is often due to over-pronation of the foot (foot rolls in at push-off).

- Front of shin – anterior shin splints. When the pain is in the muscle on the front of the lower leg, it is "anterior tibial shin splints". This is very often due to having too long a stride when running and especially when walking. Downhill terrain should be avoided as much as possible during the healing.

- Stress fracture – If the pain is in a very specific place and increases as you run, it could be a more serious problem: a stress fracture. This is unusual for beginning runners, but characteristic of those who do too much, too soon. It can also indicate low bone density. If you even suspect a stress fracture, do not run or do anything stressful on the leg and see a doctor. Stress fractures take weeks of no running, usually wearing a cast. They may also indicate a calcium deficiency.

Heel pain – Plantar fascia

"The most effective treatment is putting your foot in a supportive shoe before your first step in the morning."

This very common injury (pain on the inside or center of the heel) is felt when you first walk on the foot in the morning. As you get warmed up, it gradually goes away, only to return the next morning. The most important treatment is to put your foot in a supportive shoe before you step out of bed. Be sure to get a "shoe check" at a technical running store to make sure that you have the right shoe for your foot. This is another injury that allows for running as you heal, but stay in touch with your doctor.

If the pain is felt during the day and is noticeable, you should consult a podiatrist. Usually the doctor will construct a foot support that will surround your arch and heel. This does not always need to be a hard orthotic and is usually a softer one designed for your foot with build-ups in the right places.

The "toe squincher" exercise can help develop foot strength that will give support to the foot. It takes several weeks for this to take effect. The "squincher" is done by pointing your food down and contracting the muscles in the foot similar to making a hard "fist" with your hand.

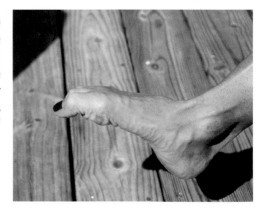

Back of the foot – Achilles tendon

The achilles tendon is the narrow band of tendons rising up from the heel and connecting to the calf muscle. It is part of a very efficient mechanical system, acting like a strong rubber band to leverage a lot of work out of the foot with a little effort from the calf muscle. It is usually injured due to excessive stretching, either through running or stretching exercises. First, avoid any activity that stretches the tendon in any way. It helps to add a small heel lift to all shoes, which reduces the range of motion. Every night, rub a chunk of ice directly on the tendon. Keep rubbing for about 15 minutes, until the tendon gets numb. Bags of ice or frozen gels don't do any good at all in my opinion. Usually, after 3-5 days off from running, the icing takes hold and gets the injury in a healing mode. Anti-inflammatory medication very rarely helps with the achilles tendon, according to experts.

Hip and groin

There are a variety of elements that could be aggravated in the hip area. Since the hips are not prime movers in running, they are usually abused when you continue to push on when very fatigued. The hips try to do the work of the leg muscles and are not designed for this. Ask your doctor about prescription strength anti-inflammatory medication, as this can often speed up recovery. Avoid stretching and any activity that aggravates the area.

Calf muscle

The calf is the most important muscle for running. It is often irritated by speedwork and can be pushed into injury by stretching, running too fast when tired, too many speed sessions without adequate rest between, and sprinting at the end of races or workouts. Bouncing too high and running a lot of hills can also trigger this injury.

Deep tissue massage has been the best treatment for most calf muscle problems. Try to find a very experienced massage therapist who has helped lots of runners with calf problems. This can be painful but is almost the only way to remove some bio-damage in the muscle. The "stick" can be very beneficial for working damage out of the calf muscle on a daily basis (see our website for more information on this product).

Don't stretch! Stretching will tear the muscle fibers that are trying to heal. Avoid running hills and take very frequent walk breaks as you return to running.

26 The Clothing Thermometer

A major source of anxiety and needless negative triggers to the reflex brain are weather and clothing concerns. There is no positive effect from worrying about the weather. It will be what it is during the race. You will gain major control over your comfort by using the table below as you prepare for any possibility on race day.

Gaining control over your clothing comfort means having available the various garments (listed below) for any combination of weather conditions during a workout or race. When packing your bag, look at every weather condition you might encounter on that day and pack your bag accordingly. At race expos, there are usually vendors of major brands, like Mizuno, in case you left something behind. The night before, lay out various combinations of garments that would be appropriate according to various weather conditions.

Get up earlier than usual on long run/race mornings when there are clothing issues and check the radar and/or forecast. The first layer, since it will be next to your skin, should feel comfortable and be designed to move moisture away from your skin. You may have to resist the temptation to buy a fashion color, but function is most important. As you try on the clothing in the store, watch for seams and extra material in areas where you will have body parts rubbing together thousands of times during a run.

Cotton is usually not a good fabric, especially for those who perspire a great deal. The cotton will absorb the sweat, hold it next to your skin and increase the weight you must carry during the run. This has also been a cause of chaffing. Garments made out of fabric labeled Breath Thermo, Polypro, Coolmax, Drifit, etc., can retain enough body heat to keep you warm in winter while releasing the extra amount. By moving moisture to the outside of the garment, you will stay cooler in summer, while avoiding the winter chill later in the year. A new fabric by Mizuno, called Breath Thermo, actually heats up with modest perspiration in the winter.

Temperature – What to Wear

14C or 60F (and above) Tank top or singlet, and shorts

9 to13C or 50 to 59F T-shirt and shorts

5 to 8C or 40 to 49F Long-sleeve light-weight shirt, shorts or tights (or nylon long pants),mittens and gloves

0 to 4C or 30 to 39F Long-sleeve medium weight shirt, and another T-shirt, tights and shorts, socks, mittens or gloves, and a hat over the ears

-4 to -1C or 20-29F Medium weight long-sleeve shirt, another T-shirt, tights and shorts, socks, mittens or gloves, and a hat over the ears

-8 to –3C or 10-19F Medium weight long-sleeve shirt, and medium/heavy weight shirt, tights and shorts, nylon wind suit, top and pants, socks, thick mittens, and a hat over the ears

-12 to –7C or 0-9F Two medium or heavyweight lon-sleeve tops, thick tights, thick underwear (especially for men), medium to heavy warm up, gloves and thick mittens, ski mask, a hat over the ears, and Vaseline covering any exposed skin.

-18 to –11C or –15F Two heavyweight long-sleeve tops, tights and thick tights, thick underwear (and supporter for men), thick warm up (top and pants), mittens over gloves, thick ski mask and a hat over ears, Vasoline covering any exposed skin, thicker socks on your feet and other foot protection, as needed.

Minus 20 both C & F Add layers as needed

What Not to Wear

1. A heavy coat in winter. If the layer is too thick, you'll heat up, sweat excessively, and cool too much when you take it off.
2. No shirt for men in summer. Fabric that holds some of the moisture will give you more of a cooling effect as you run and walk.
3. Too much sun screen – it can interfere with sweating.
4. Socks that are too thick in summer. Your feet swell and the pressure from the socks can increase the chance of a black toenail and blisters.
5. Lime green shirt with bright pink polka dots (unless you have a lot of confidence and/or can run fast).

Special cases

Chaffing can be reduced by lycra and other fabric. Many runners have eliminated chaffing between the legs by using a lycra "bike tight" as an undergarment. These are also called "lycra shorts." There are also several skin lubricants on the market, including Glide.

Some men suffer from irritation of their nipples. Having a slick and smooth fabric across the chest will reduce this. There is now a product called Nip-Guard that has reduced the chance of having this problem.

28 Products that Enhance Running

HydraPouch – Your chance to do something "green"

This is the only company I know of that is trying to eliminate the waste produced by cups and plastic bottles at races. The pouch cost about $15, clips to the band on your shorts and can be refilled as you move from water fountain, to water station, or loops around the neighborhood. The company has patented a valve, attached to a conventional water jug, that will fill up the pouch in one second. This is not a carrying container like a fuel belt or Camelback. I endorse HydraPouch, and the reduction of waste that it stands for (www.hydrapouch.com or www.jeffgalloway.com).

Nite Beams – To light up the darkness

This company has various light products that make you more visible when running after dark. The bands can go around arms or legs, and either blink or stay lit. There is a ring that blinks and is quite bright. They are also developing a headlamp product in a visor or ball cap that lights up the path ahead (www.nitebeams.com or www.jeffgalloway.com).

The Stick

This massage tool can help the muscles recover quicker. It will often speed up the recovery of muscle injuries or iliotibial band injuries (on the outside of the upper leg, between knee and hip). This type of device can help warm up the leg muscles and sore tendons before running, and move some of the waste out afterward.

In working on the calf muscle (most important in running) start each stroke at the achilles tendon and roll up the leg toward the knee. Gently roll back to the origin and continue repeatedly. For the first 5 minutes, your gentle rolling will bring additional blood flow to the area. As you gradually increase the pressure on the calf, you will usually find some "knots" or sore places in the muscles. Concentrate on these as you roll over them again and again, breaking up the tightness. See www.RunInjuryFree. com for more info on this.

Foam Roller – Self-massage for I-T Band, hip, etc.

The most popular size of this cylinder is about 6" in diameter and one foot long. This has been the most successful treatment device for iliotibial band injury. In treating this injury, put the roller on the floor and lie on you side so that the irritated I-T band area is on top of the roller. As your body weight presses down on the roller, roll up and down on the area of the leg you want to treat. Roll gently for 2-3 minutes and then let the body weight press down more.

This is a very effective pre-warm-up exercise for any area that needs more blood flow as you start. It is also very beneficial to use the roller after a run on the same areas. See www.RunInjuryFree.com for more info on this product.

Endurox Excel

An hour before a long or hard workout, I take two of these Excel pills. Among the antioxidants is the active ingredient from ginseng: ciwega. Research has shown that recovery speeds up when this product is taken. I also use it when my legs have been more tired than usual for 2-3 days in a row.

Accelerade

This sports drink has a patented formula shown to improve recovery. It also helps to improve hydration. I recommend having some in the refrigerator as your fluid intake product taken throughout the day. The prime time to drink this regularly is the day before and after a long or strenuous workout day. During a prolonged speed training session, have a thermos nearby for sipping on walk breaks.

Research has also shown that drinking Accelerade about 30 minutes before running can get the body's start-up fuel (glycogen) activated more effectively and may conserve the limited supply of this crucial fuel. For a discount on this product, go to www.JeffGalloway.com, and click on the "Accelerade" link.

Endurox R4

This product has what I see as a "cult following" among runners. In fact, the research shows that the 4-1 ratio of carbohydrate to protein helps to reload the muscle glycogen more quickly. This means that the muscles feel bouncy and ready to do what you can do sooner. There are other antioxidants that speed recovery. The prime time for this reloading process is within 30 minutes of the finish of a run. For a discount on this product, go to www.JeffGalloway.com, and click on the "Endurox" link.

Other Galloway Books: Training Schedules and Gifts that Keep on Giving – Even to Yourself

(Order them, autographed, from www.JeffGalloway.com)

Year-round Plan

This is my most comprehensive training book. It has all of the elements scheduled, leading to goal races of 5K, 10K, half marathon and marathon, within 52 weeks. It weaves the training for several races at one time.

Boston – How to Qualify

Training is listed for each of the qualifying times for Boston. You'll find a listing of the courses that have produced the highest percentage of Boston qualifying finishers. My friend Bill Rodgers (4-time Boston champion) helped me provide a guide on how to run the Boston course. There are several enhanced training tips to maximize performance that are not included in other books, along with nutrition, motivation, and lots of other information.

Cross Country

This is a complete guide for training and racing "off road" for 5K, 2 mile and 1 mile. There are sections on team strategies, mental training, nutrition, recovery, and much more.

Galloway Marathon FAQs

There are over 100 of the most common questions I receive about marathon training and racing. You don't have to wade through pages of text to get the answers to your questions.

Running Until You're 100

In the chapter on joint health, you'll see in the research studies that runners have healthier joints than sedentary folks. In the chapter on the researched health benefits of exercise, an expert on longevity says that for every hour we exercise we can expect to get back 2 hours of life extension. Among the heroes section is an 85-year-old who recently finished his 700th marathon and will do 29 more in one year. There are nutrition suggestions from Nancy Clark, training adjustments by decade, and many other helpful hints for running past the century mark.

Fit Kids – Smarter Kids

This book is a handbook for parents, teachers, and youth leaders to how to lead kids into fitness that is fun. A growing number of studies are listed that document how kids who exercise do better in academics and in life. Nancy Clark gives tips on what to eat, and there's a chapter on childhood obesity, with the hope that others, like the author (a former fat kid), can turn things around. There are resources, successful programs, inspirational stories and much more.

A Woman's Guide to Running & A Woman's Guide to Walking

By Barbara and Jeff Galloway.

The section on woman-specific issues makes this book unique: pregnancy, menstrual issues, bra-fitting, incontinence, osteoporosis, inner organs shifting, menopause and more. There's a section for the unique problems of the "fabulously full figured" runners. Nutrition, fat-burning, motivation, starting up, aches and pains – all are covered in the book. There's also a section in each book written by famous sports nutritionist Nancy Clark.

A Woman's Guide to Fat Burning

By Barbara and Jeff Galloway. I've not seen another book that better describes the fat burning and accumulation process with a strategy to take action. There are several important and inexpensive tools mentioned with recipes and specific suggestions about managing calorie income and expenditure. There is also a section on women-specific issues.

Walking

Walkers now have a book that explains the many benefits, how to maximize them, with training programs for 5K, 10K, half and full marathons. There is resource information on fat-burning, nutrition, motivation and much more.

Getting Started

This is more than a state-of-the-art book for beginners. It gently takes walkers into running with a 6-month schedule that has been very successful. Also included is information on fat-burning, nutrition, motivation, and body management. This is a great gift for your friends or relatives who can be "infected" positively by running.

Prevention and Care of Running Injuries

Dave Hannaford is one of the best resources I've found in explaining why we get injured and how to heal. He breaks down each major running injury to help you diagnose, treat and heal. I have written the section on prevention, based upon more than 30 years of no overuse injuries.

A Year-Round Plan

You'll find daily workouts for 52 weeks, for three levels of runners: to finish, to maximize potential, and time improvement. It has long runs, speed sessions, drills, hill sessions, all listed, in the order needed to do a 5K, 10K, half and marathon during one year. Resource material is included to help with many running issues.

Galloway's Book On Running 2nd Edition

This is the best-seller among running books since 1984. Thoroughly revised and expanded in 2001, you'll find training programs for 5K, 10K, half marathon, with nutrition, fat-burning, walk breaks, motivation, injuries, shoes, and much more. This is a total resource book.

Marathon – You Can Do It (Revised)

This has the latest marathon training and racing information. It was revised in 2010.

Galloway Training Programs

This has the information you need to train for the classic event, the marathon. But it also has schedules for half marathon and 10 mile. This has the latest on walk breaks, long runs, practical nutrition, the "magic mile", mental marathon toughness and much more.

Testing Yourself

Training programs for 1 mile, 2 mile, 5K, and 1.5 mile are detailed, along with information on racing-specific information in nutrition, mental toughness, running form. There are also some very accurate prediction tests that allow you to tell what is a realistic goal. This book has been used effectively by those who are stuck in a performance rut at 10K or longer events. By training and racing faster, you can improve running efficiency and your tolerance for waste products, like lactic acid.

Half Marathon

This new book provides highly successful and detailed training schedules for various time goals for this important running goal. Information is provided on nutrition, mental preparation, fluids, race day logistics & check list, and much more.

5K-10K

Whether you want to finish with a smile on your face, or have a challenging time goal in mind, this book is a total resource for these distances. There are schedules for a wide range of performances, how to eat, how to predict your performance, how long and how fast to run on long runs, drills to improve form and speed training. There is extensive information on mental preparation, breaking through barriers, practical nutrition and more.

Jeff Galloway's Training Journal

Some type of journal is recommended to organize and track your training plan. *Jeff Galloway's Training Journal* can be ordered from www.JeffGalloway.com, autographed. It simplifies the process with places to fill in information for each day. There is also space for recording the unexpected thoughts and experiences that make so many runs come alive again as we read them.

- **Running Schools and Retreats**

  Jeff conducts motivating running schools and retreats. These feature individualized information, form evaluation, comprehensively covering running, nutrition, and fat burning.

- **NextFit – Coaching Through the iPod**

  As an extension of Jeff's training programs, he has teamed up with Podfitness.com to bring these workouts into your daily life. Now you can have a custom program, during which Jeff coaches you through every training session on your iPod.

"My Podfitness training program is designed to reinforce what you've read here. Your program is designed expressly for you and changes with you. You'll hear me throughout your workout, offering advice and encouragement. Plus, it lays your music in the background, which I think makes each run even more enjoyable." – JG

Go to www.Jeffgalloway.com and click on the NextFit link.

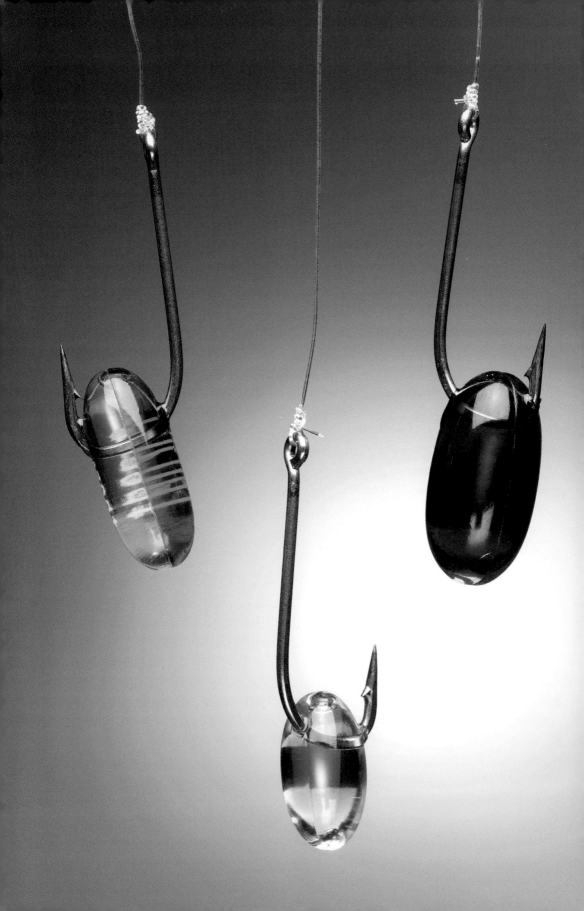

Vitamins

I now believe that most runners need a good vitamin to help the immune system and resist infection. There is some evidence that getting the proper vitamin mix can speed recovery. The vitamin line I use is called Cooper Complete. Dr. Kenneth Cooper is behind this product. In the process of producing the best body of research on exercise and long-term health I've seen anywhere, he found that certain vitamins help in many ways.

Buffered Salt Tablets to Reduce Cramping

If your muscles cramp on long or hard runs, this type of product may help greatly. The buffered sodium and potassium tablets get into the system more quickly. Be sure to ask your doctor if this product is OK for you (those with high blood pressure, especially). If you are taking a statin drug for cholesterol and are cramping, it is doubtful that this will help. Ask your doctor about adjusting the medication before long runs.

28 Credit Where Credit Is Due

I was fortunate to have been taught by some great teachers and thinkers at Westminster Schools in Atlanta and Wesleyan University (CT). In many classes, I debated the issue of whether genetics or environment was the primary influence on human behavior and evolution. While I have always acknowledged the opportunity of an individual to make choices, the paradigm of my educational experience (1960s) predicted that genetics and DNA were the primary determinant in behavior. Human evolution, according to many thinkers in the '60s, was creating a rift between mind and body. Genetically, brains could do amazing things, producing a separation from the primitive instincts of the body. The trend seemed to be clear: If we had the right genetics, our mind would be capable of navigating us thorough life, while the frailties of the body could divert us from our potential. So the concept was that of a hierarchical structure of the brain dictating what the body should do. Then came volumes of research showing that this was not the case.

My experience in my career has shown me that those who seemingly had no physical ability and led sedentary and unfulfilled lives for years have turned their lives around by setting an endurance goal using running and walking. Over more than 35 years, I've heard thousands of success stories, and I've come to believe that most of us can gain control over our attitude and find inside ourselves the motivation we need to stay on track, overcome challenges, or break through barriers.

During the past 10 years, my wife Barbara has introduced me to the work of others who have come to similar conclusions and explained the biological reasons behind these changes. In several sections of this book, I have referred to the work of Bruce Lipton, PhD, Candace Pert, PhD, and John Sarno, MD. Each has made major contributions in scientifically documenting how the mind and body are embedded, and how individuals can change behavior patterns. Since we are, to a great extent, what we do and what we think about, the choices we make each day determine who we are and what we will become.

Dr. Lipton is a cellular biologist who has conducted landmark research on how genes are controlled by an individual's perception of the environment. When mind, body, and spirit are focused on change, a process of evolution can bring it about.

Dr. Candace Pert conducted breakthrough research while at the National Institutes of Health, Georgetown University Medical Center and other institutions. She discovered the cellular receptors for endorphins and explained the information network of hormones throughout the body, which respond to our beliefs and thoughts.

Dr. John Sarno has spent a career helping people overcome orthopedic problems through understanding TMS (tension myositis syndrome). His vast clinical experience with a very high cure rate has shown that a significant percentage of individuals with chronic pain are suffering from the effects of stress, which triggers an unconscious reduction of blood flow to damaged areas.

I endorse the following books and highly recommend them:

Biology of Belief, by Bruce Lipton, PhD, Hay House, Inc., 2005

Molecules of Emotions ,by Candace B. Pert, PhD, Scribner, 1997

The Mind-body Connection ,by John E. Sarno, MD, Wellness Central, 1998

Photo Credits:

Inside Pages:

Page 10:	Nikolay Grygoryev/Relay/www.thinkstock.de
Page 14:	carmeneve/Marathon Motion Blur/www.thinkstock.de
Page 17:	Brand X Pictures/Woman running/www.thinkstock.de
Page 20:	Jupiterimages/Marathon/www.thinkstock.de
Page 24:	Stockbyte/Man and Woman Jogging in Park/www.thinkstock.de
Page 28:	Stockbyte/Young man yelling/www.thinkstock.de
Page 32:	Hande Guleryuz Yuce/To Do List/www.thinkstock.de
Page 36:	Ken Vander Putten/Finish Line/www.thinkstock.de
Page 40/41:	Tibor Nagy/Marathon Runners/www.thinkstock.de
Page 42:	Jupiterimages/© 2006 Mehmet G.Emin/www.thinkstock.de
Page 49:	Tony Sanchez/Muscular man jogging/www.thinkstock.de
Page 50:	Stockbyte/Man and Woman Jogging/www.thinkstock.de
Page 62:	Jupiterimages/Athletic Man Resting after Race/www.thinkstock.de
Page 72:	Jupiterimages/www.thinkstock.de
Page 80:	Tibor Nagy/Runners/www.thinkstock.de
Page 82:	Hemera Technologies/Marathon Runners Jogging Over Bridge/www.thinkstock.de
Page 87:	Alan Bailey/A Young Woman is Squatting Down/www.thinkstock.de
Page 88:	Jupiterimages/Runners in Marathon Race/www.thinkstock.de
Page 89:	Petr Gnuskin/Stil-Life with Notebook/www.thinkstock.de
Page 90:	Autor/Training-Journal
Page 94:	Bob Ingelhart/Young Man Jogging/www.thinkstock.de

Page 104:	Pixland/Athletes Crouching at Starting Line/www.thinkstock.de
Page 106:	Karl Weatherly/Man Jogging on Trail by Trees in Mountain Area/www.thinkstock.de
Page 109:	BananaStock/Person Using Treadmill/www.thinkstock.de
Page 116:	Ryan McVay/Four Men Jogging on Beach/www.thinkstock.de
Page 120:	Polka Dot Images/Runners at Starting Line/www.thinkstock.de
Page 124:	Mark Hunt/Two Teenage Boys Running/www.thinkstock.de
Page 132:	Unknown/Running Girl/www.thinkstock.de
Page 134:	Irena Misevic/Man with Knee Pain/www.thinkstock.de
Page 136:	Hemera Technologies/Physical therapy/www.thinkstock.de
Page 138:	Jupiterimages/Woman Putting On Knee Brace/www.thinkstock.de
Page 139:	Jeff Galloway
Page 140:	Jeff Galloway
Page 142:	Jupiterimages/Man Joggin in Field/www.thinkstock.de
Page 144:	Unknown/www.thinkstock.de
Page 150:	Unknown/Marathon Hamburg 2006/www.thinkstock.de
Page 154:	Jeffrey Hamilton/Capsules on Fishing Hooks/www.thinkstock.de
Page 156:	Unknown/Person Holding a Stop Watch in Front of a Runner Ready to Start a Race/www.thinkstock.de

Cover Design:	Sabine Groten
Cover Photo:	Imago
Jacket Photos:	Tibor Nagy/Marathon Runners/www.thinkstock.de
	Hemera Technologies/Marathon Runners Jogging Over Bridge/www.thinkstock.de

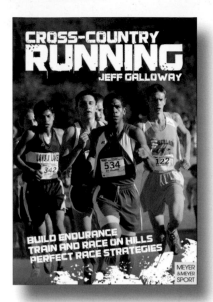
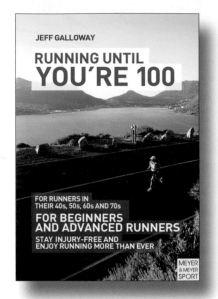
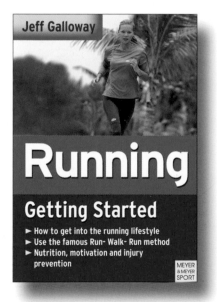
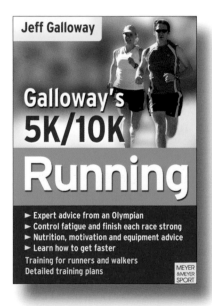